REBIRTHING BREATHWORK

The making of an independent adult

by
Catherine Holland

ISBN 978-0-9521696-4-2

Cover photograph by Gary Cunnington.

REBIRTHING BREATHWORK:
The making of an independent adult

By Catherine Holland

. . .

www.catherineholland.co.uk

Dedicated to my children,
Anna, Rebecca and Peter
for growing up into such fine people

• • •

PREFACE To the Third Edition

Eighteen years have now passed since I wrote the first Introduction to Rebirthing Breathwork. In the second edition I decided to add observations about child rearing that I hope you will find relevant; either because you are raising children or because they help to explain why many of us continue to be so needy into adulthood. Then I hope that you will join me in aspiring to maturity, to rise to a level of acceptance where we know that we are valued and we do not have to compete, in a generous Universe where there is plenty for all of us.

This is all my opinion, based on observation and experience. I have had the benefit of giving birth to children, sharing their growing up, learning from their realisations and finally knowing them as adults - reflecting on their childhood. Also I have been privileged to share in the development of my rebirthing clients; they teach me so much about the effect of parenting practice. I invite you to share in learning from all those around us, especially our children.

In the third edition, I have added my conclusions after writing about my accident where my leg was crushed by a car and I nearly died, and why it was that I was able to *decide* not to.

January 2016

CONTENTS

Introduction

Introduction

Over the last few years so many people have suggested that I write a book that I have at last taken the hint and begun. I have learned so much and it seems that what I have learned is also useful to others. Much of this has been through bringing up my children (and from them) and from the realisation that we are all children inside forever ... Now when I meet someone I can sense and see a complete person with a depth that was not apparent to me before. I have noticed that there is a method in the way to go about this and I would like to share it with you - so, here goes.

When I was a child I felt that there was a magical element to life which was actually an important part of the way that the Universe worked, but it was a secret because it was not discussed. I have read widely and observed people carefully as an adult and I know that what I felt as a child is true. The reawakening of that belief is exciting - it means that whoever chooses to can experience wonder, joy and understanding in their everyday life; even in a society that has carefully ignored the innate wisdom in everyone, to know what is right for them and the ability to achieve it.

After studying Psychology for a year I realised that nobody is right, that all studies are subjective, and also that everyone knows what is true for them. I did not feel comfortable with any of the therapeutic methods I came across; they were superficial because they relied on intellectual argument and change to try to alter an emotional experience. Although someone will feel better temporarily, from the attention being paid to them during the time spent in discussion of their circumstances, it does not resolve anything, and sooner or later this lack of resolution will make the visits to their advisor seem pointless. So I carried on reading and I brought up a family - learning the best way to do this from them as I went (more of this later) with this interest at the back of my mind. Eventually I found an excellent method of emotional resolution because I really needed one: it is Conscious Connected Breathing, known as Rebirthing breathwork.

... 1 ...
REBIRTHING BREATHWORK

When we have had frightening experiences, without the necessary help and support to feel safe, during our lives the stress remains with us but we block out the memory. This leaves us with a feeling of anxiety and uncertainty. We know that frightening things happen, but we can't learn from them, because we have buried the experience in order to avoid the fear or pain - which overwhelmed us at the time as we felt unsupported.

As adults, many of us have fears of circumstances that are clearly remnants of childhood, e.g. fear of the dark or of living alone. We put up with conditions that we do not like at all to avoid the greater fear. When we trace back and resolve that original fear we can take control of the present. Rebirthing breathwork is a good way to do this.

What a Rebirthing Breathwork session is like

During a breathwork session, as your Rebirther, I ask you to lie down on a mattress on the floor and relax taking long, full, deep breaths.

I then guide you through an hour or so of circular breathing - where one breath joins the next without pause. I may encourage you to leave everyday cares behind by visualisation, of somewhere real or imaginary, which allows feelings about other experiences to emerge. (The majority of Westerners breath in a limited way - about half our waking hours - and this new way of breathing releases thoughts that we have suppressed, by mimicking the chemical conditions in the body when we first experienced them. This can feel threatening, which is why we breathe in this way at first with someone there. Once you feel confident that you can handle your fears from the past on your own, you are ready to Rebirth yourself alone. Then the technique continues to be useful whenever you need it, for ever.)

I will encourage you to open your life to change, perhaps repeating an affirmation for you (see appendix) that is relevant to the particular issues that we have discussed before your breathing session. I am often guided by my intuition to what is a pressing issue for clients - a welcome change in my own life that I have developed. It is important that you feel safe and free to express fears that may seem silly - this is part of the process of understanding conclusions reached early in life, when as children we may never have been given adequate explanations for events and got the impression we were stupid for not knowing: it can be an enormous relief to realise that we were not to blame for being young and not knowing everything we felt we were supposed to. I am often asked "Is this normal?"

about the common misunderstandings we feel somehow relate only to us.

I direct a change in the pace and style of breathing when it seems that this would help to release tension and thoughts. I will ask you to concentrate on breathing into the upper part of your chest to release emotions. The chest (the muscles used for breathing) often carries considerable tension, because we hold our breath when we are upset or afraid. If we do not then relax completely the tension remains with us, and we carry it forever: this is tiring, and the chronic tension of muscles contributes to various conditions requiring medical treatment. While Rebirthing, these tensions become more obvious as the rest of your body relaxes; continuing to breathe regularly during the tension allows it to be released - sometimes dramatically, with a sense of enormous relief and pleasure after such a long time under stress.

It is useful to discover as much as you can about the details of your birth. There are similarities in the lives and feelings of people who have had, for example, the same medical intervention during their birth, and it can speed up the process of understanding and acceptance of your life as it is. Once acceptance is achieved the process of change can begin - it helps to know where we are starting from before we begin our journey. If you cannot find out details about your birth they will emerge anyway during Rebirths, but a useful way to find out about something you cannot consciously remember is to draw upon your store of 'general conclusions about life' by writing out "Birth is: " and writing out what comes into your head, do it about 20 times. This will give you a good idea of what your experience of birth in your life has been (remembering that it will also have been influenced by the general opinion of society). I also lend my clients books; I find it reinforces our own discoveries about life when others have independently come to the same conclusions.

During a Rebirth you will re-experience those times which you were unable to deal with satisfactorily the first time around, when you will feel emotions - confusion, pain, sadness - that you blocked off the first time, unable to accept them. (Because you couldn't deal with them, you pretended they didn't exist. We genuinely believe that we do not experience the emotions of which we are not aware, and we need to understand the desirability of feeling the full range of emotions and the advantage of making the effort to do this - so that the effort is worthwhile in our opinion. I cannot make you feel anything you do not wish to or are afraid of, and it is counterproductive to try to do so. We are afraid because of previous experience - we have been hurt before - but you can find the safety of a trusting relationship when you see the desirability of change; and you wouldn't have read this far if you thought it was all a waste of time.) Now they will become a part of your continuum of experience, accepted as part of your life that you have learned from and put behind you. They no longer hold any threat or require effort to suppress them, so life feels easier and more relaxed. You become more open and understanding with other people as you are less afraid to express how you feel; you no longer have the idea that you are stupid if you need to ask for information or help, and you expect your opinions to be listened to. This process of accepting your past experiences and your feelings about them into your everyday life is called Integration.

I will draw the session to a conclusion by making you aware of your surroundings and lessening your concentration on your breath. We will then discuss your experience, what you felt, thought and remembered. Once the issues that have arisen today are dealt with you can go back to your daily life satisfactorily. The sensations do stay for a while, some of the permanent changes are profound and immediately apparent, some take longer to be revealed. A breath release is an example of an immediate effect. A group of chest muscles relax suddenly in unison, the chest capacity increases and you feel energised and elated for several days until you get used to the new state. Subtler changes may be that you are able to sleep better or go out in the cold air without suffering shortness of breath.

People usually book 10 sessions at weekly intervals to learn to Rebirth themselves; however the number can vary. Each session lasts about two and a half hours altogether.

... 2 ...
USES OF REBIRTHING BREATHWORK

Rebirthing breathwork encourages us to discover and challenge our limiting beliefs and thoughts. It reveals our inner wisdom to us and often during a breathwork session we have new ideas.

It reveals our inner capabilities which we may have been unaware of.

It gives us courage.

It helps us to tell the truth fast.

It allows physical symptoms to heal/be healed.

It enables us to be ourselves.

It enriches our relationships.

It improves our opinion of ourselves.

I believe one of the greatest services I have to offer is the improvement of the quality of someone's life while they are alone. It is a good measure of your happiness and self-worth if you are comfortable enjoying time on your own (especially if you have always needed company before).

Rebirthing frees us from the need for compulsive behaviours and addictions: these are used to cover needs that are unfulfilled by suppressing uncomfortable feelings. In this way we can become aware of our body's ability to let us know what it needs:

natural foods, exercise, touch, fresh air. We can tune in to what our body needs because we can feel it at last - what a relaxed body always does. When we are no longer using tremendous amounts of energy to suppress our feelings, we have a natural liveliness and no need for the artificial boost from white sugar and chocolate (we can still eat for fun and enjoyment, we just don't have the compulsion/dependence). Relaxed muscles are sensitive because they are soft when not in use: permanently tensed muscles are hard, unyielding and tired. The release of the energy no longer needed to keep these muscles tense can be used to make us more aware of the predicament and needs of others. So we become nicer to know and more approachable when we rid ourselves of the mental burdens we carry. Other people notice this faster than we do, in common with others I have had a different reaction from those around me since I started Rebirthing.

... 3 ...

THE PRINCIPLES OF REBIRTHING

Rebirthing is often described as having five elements:

I	Circular Breathing
II	Awareness
III	Integration
IV	Relaxation
V	Uniqueness/Whatever You Do is Right for You

I Circular Breathing

The Rebirthing breath is a relaxed, flowing breath where one breath joins the next without pause. It sometimes helps to visualise a circle or an infinity symbol being outlined in your mind to keep the continuity. It gets easier with practice, and it is useful to have a Rebirther with you until you have learned to recognise your breathing pattern yourself. If you keep breathing, you cannot suppress emotion: that's how we suppress - by controlling our breathing. The next principles then follow on as a matter of course if the connected breathing is continued.

II Awareness

While you are lying down and learning the breathing technique you will be asked to notice any bodily sensations (tingling, tightness etc.) and thoughts that come to mind (memories, ideas etc.) without judgement. Observing in this way while still breathing continually enables you to acknowledge all feelings old and new.

III Integration

You need to be willing to allow yourself to feel without judgement, to accept the present experience without comparing it with past experience, or worrying about what it may lead to in the future. This means that you keep breathing during uncomfortable, unhappy or powerful feelings. Once your feelings are being acknowledged and perhaps expressed - maybe for the first time - you are able to absorb them into your life experience.

IV Relaxation

Integration leads to relaxation as part of the process, an end product. At the beginning, the amount of Relaxation at your conscious command may be limited; it is part of being open to change - willing to allow yourself to feel, no longer to label your feelings as wrong, thereby shutting them in with tension. There is often an enormous sense of relief and pleasure at this point, as if an enormous burden had been put down. You my feel more relaxed than you have ever felt, and very happy.

V Uniqueness/Whatever You Do is Right for You

No two Breathwork sessions are ever the same. I don't know what issue a client will choose to deal with today (and neither do they) when they breathe; it is not important for us to know. I trust the process and the client's Inner Self to know exactly what's right for them, as much or as little as they are ready to work with at this point. It takes a certain amount of courage to delve into the unknown and I acknowledge everyone for that; remember, your Rebirther has been through all this and has, at times, felt similar.

Twenty Breaths Exercise

This is an exercise using the connected breath that you can practise at any time. It is good for relaxing before you go to sleep. Practising this exercise daily will begin to change your breathing. Try it now:

Four short breaths, one long breath. Repeat four times (twenty altogether).

Connect the inbreath and outbreath with no pauses between them at all.

... 4 ...

BIRTH THE FIRST TIME AROUND

The Human Body is superbly designed to carry out its function efficiently and flexibly. The physiology of birth is fascinating and precise; it is designed to work under normal conditions of gravity and movement that the body is accustomed to. It also runs in sequence, one stage interlocking hormonally and physically with the next. Few civilised peoples can resist the temptation (wherever it came from) to interfere with the process at some point, apparently unaware of the destruction they may cause to the delicately balanced (and tried and tested) system, that works with such reliability when allowed to run its natural course. (Even the position of birthing may be dictated, which can have huge implications. The position a woman should give birth in is best chosen by the woman at the time ... and even if the birth is not interfered with Western women are usually so afraid that the baby is too.) Unfortunately so few of us are aware of that natural course, and afraid because of our lack of knowledge and trust, that we rely on those who have set themselves up as experts (or whom we have set up), and may only realise afterwards the drawbacks of intervention.

Those doing the intervening are not responsible for the care of mothers and babies later, so the consequences usually pass unaccounted for. The women do not see the same medical personnel again, the babies are not articulate enough to voice their opinion to insensitive adults who don't realise they have an opinion. The conclusion that the women and society come to is that there are consequences in terms of ill-health and psychological damage that are normal consequences of birthing and that their bodies are badly designed ...

Ideally, when a baby is first born, it is held gently while it experiments with taking its first tentative breaths, and rests a little until it is confidently breathing. This may take a few minutes, or it may take half an hour. During this time, the placenta is still working and there is no urgency about the baby breathing independently. It is usual for nature to make sure that there is a wide overlap of two life support systems at a time of changeover. In this way, the baby learns to breathe in a state of relaxation and safety, and carries on breathing in this way for the rest of its life. The standard Western practice of removing the baby from its mother and cutting the cord immediately catapults the baby into using an untried system in a state of emergency. The delicate lining of the baby's lungs is used suddenly in a state of panic and fear for the first time, with no choice but to breathe or die. The life line has already been cut off. The combination of being removed from the place of familiarity (the mother) and having the reliable source of oxygen cut off at a time of enormous natural stress is too much for a baby to take calmly in its stride.

This is the way most of us have been brought into the world. It is no wonder that we find breathing tense and unpleasant, and believe life is unsafe.

... 5 ...

WHAT A BABY NEEDS TO BE A COMPLETE AND COMPETENT INDIVIDUAL
- but you probably didn't get ...

FROM THE MOMENT I COULD TALK I WAS ORDERED TO LISTEN

Cat Stevens: Father and Son

To be held constantly (at first, later when he asks)
To be fed at anytime
To be trusted to know what is right for himself
To be listened to
To be given what he needs
To be accepted just the way he is
To have the rules explained in a way that he understands when he is ready
To be a part of everyday life which goes on around him
To be told the truth
To be respected as a whole person; complete, just small

It was tough to follow my instinct when those around me felt it was peculiar to want to carry my baby with me, but I felt it was the right thing to do, and I know many women who reluctantly ignored their instincts, followed the advice of others about the rearing of their own babies and have regretted it.

The effort involved in the caring for a young baby is often seen as an unrewarding and thankless task. People have asked me about how tiring it is to carry a bonny baby consistently; it is a joy and such a lovely thing to do, I recommend it. I used to have back trouble years ago and realised how wanting to do this influenced my body. I realised after carrying each of my children on my back for several years (for some part of the day) that I had never had trouble carrying a warm, snugly, heavy weight on my back.

Women have said they tried it but found the baby too heavy - their expectation that it will be tiring? (See 'The Continuum Concept' for ideas on the attitudes we have to the carrying of burdens.) It takes persistence, a well-designed carrier and experimentation. I found the use of it on the back is so much easier. I feel sad that we are not prepared well so that it is not so hard to care for our own children - women would love to enjoy it, men too.

The language used about babies in our society gives away the general consensus of opinion about them e.g. "Demand Feeding"- suggesting an onerous burden for the mother, or an autocratic baby; "Comfort Sucking" - used to suggest that if a baby has had enough to eat it has no right to continue sucking just for the pleasure (in fact this view is incorrect - this sucking does have a physiological purpose, to order more milk for tomorrow). It is sad that to give generously to one's own young is seen in this way and can only be an indication of a species that is not at peace with itself. It is educational to watch the parenting of other mammals toward their young, and towards the young of other species - how tolerant some dogs can be towards a baby who consistently experiments with pulling its tail or ears. It is also intriguing to see what lengths human adults will go to in tending the young of other species when they may have no patience with their own. Some explanation for this is seen in the adult's view of himself as a child and the way he was treated at the time by his parents. We tend to perpetuate the way we were reared as children when we bring up our own. This a "Learned Instinct" - something we were exposed to so early in our life. We are not aware that everyone doesn't think in exactly the same way. It can be quite a shock to realise that all families are not like our own, to see that we may not like the way our own behaves and treats other family members, and how hard it is to break the pattern despite our own best endeavours. It has indeed become instinctive; we do these things outside our conscious awareness, e.g. criticising our children for doing things that we were told not to do, when we may not personally object to those habits at all, or worrying about what other people think when we would really love our children to have the freedom to be individuals. It takes some time and a good deal of questioning our basic motives before we can admit that what we were told was the best way to lead our lives doesn't work for us and is not what we would choose to do. Our ideas about working for a living often have underlying hidden messages about not having a right to enjoy what we do for a living or working hard being the only way to earn a lot of money. When we question these objectively we may realise that this is not true for us, or not even generally true. Part of the problem is that we have been taught not to trust our own judgement and it then becomes very difficult to work out what our opinion is.

We have also been taught that a baby cannot communicate its needs, so we are blind to the messages that it tries to give us. We have only been made aware of the gross messages that we cannot ignore - like the screaming of a distressed baby after all his subtler means of communication have been misunderstood. There are places in the world where babies do not need to cry because their needs are tended to quickly. A satisfied baby is a pleasure and not a full-time occupation. My son cried a handful of times in his first few years; the only thing that really upset him was loud, unexpected noise.

We need to question the way we are bringing up our children, e.g. whether we believe that waking in the night is really such a dreadful thing to happen if a sick child needs us (adults deliberately lose sleep for other reasons), but also: whether the accepted idea of the way things are done is the only way. Westerners have invented some new ideas about what to expect from an age-old phenomenon; leaving a young mammal alone, when it is biologically designed to be accompanied, is bound to be a frustrating business - especially for the frightened baby. Some young mammals have evolved to be left: deer and hares for example, leave their young in a safe place sometimes for long periods; their milk is designed with this expectation in mind, to sustain the young animal until its mother returns. The young are born in a more mature state if this is expected of them. It is not expected of primate babies. Our milk is designed to be given at frequent intervals (half to two hourly) with the expectation that it should be available at any time, which isn't unreasonable if you are carrying the baby anyway. It begins to get tricky when you try to fit it into the society we are currently dealing with. The idea that babies can be fed infrequently and left for long periods was mooted by a man who had been studying cattle and felt that it would be good for their characters - teaching them to wait.

... 6 ...

WHAT A CHILD NEEDS AND WHAT WE OFTEN LEARN INSTEAD AS WE GROW UP

EVERYONE ALWAYS DOES THEIR BEST

To know that you are proud of him
To know that you will give him what he needs
To know that you will provide boundaries suitable to his stage of development
To know that you trust him and value his opinion
To feel useful.
Kindness (without being soppy or condescending)
To know the truth and that his parents are being true to themselves
To have wholesome natural food available and self determination about his choice of when and what to eat (to eat for his own needs rather than to suit or please others)
To be able to depend on your affection, love and support even when you disagree with his choices - it's his life
To have you available for advice, to go and sort out problems he may have with other people, to listen
To get to know you
To have his inner drive respected and allowed to remain intact
To be able to experiment and to have a place to climb

and exercise

To develop his independence at his own pace

To be spoken to with respect, thanked and apologised to when appropriate

How much of that did you get as you were growing up? Unfortunately many parents are not emotionally mature themselves - in some ways it seems odd that the physical body carries on maturing whether the emotional maturity is on a par with it or not. Having said that, gross immaturity is easy to observe because it does have an obvious physical reflection; it follows therefore that there are physical signs of emotional immaturity and we need to sharpen our powers of observation to detect them. I do feel that I can now recognise the inner person from the outer body. Some of this due to the greater sensitivity I have gained from the changes in my own life and personality, some of it from bitter experience!

> Carrying on into later life, when do we cease being a child in the eyes of our parents? When do we appear to be able to make decisions for ourselves? When do they trust us to run our own lives?
> What makes me happy? Do they have any idea? Is that what I am supposed to be asking for: their view of a suitable partner for me?

What may have happened to your parents as they grew up?

It is helpful to be able to see the difficulties our parents had but it does not remove the lack of caring we felt at the time, and we need to feel justified in our disappointment and anger that we did not get what we needed. Our needs are not related to our parents' ability to give. We need to accept the point we have reached in order to proceed. So, it is useful to consider the everyday words and actions of our upbringing - your parents may still be talking to you like that today, No wonder you'd sometimes rather not visit them. Things said to us many times throughout our upbringing are the basis for our beliefs about ourselves and our capabilities. They run like a tape in our heads: we hear them in our inner voices criticising and cajoling (or encouraging and supporting), we have absorbed their truths as our own, they form our reality, our yardstick to measure new experiences and because they are always there we do not question them.

Once we see our parents as other humans with problems - and parents of their own, we can observe their coping mechanisms based on the ideas about the best way to live their lives, given to them by their parents. It is sometimes illuminating to think about the conditions in our parents' lives when we were conceived and very young babies - and their parents in turn because we can then see what was important then may not be so any longer. Their lives may have been ruled by the restrictions of wartime, or religions which do not presently affect us, but to understand them explains why our parents were the way they were. The next step is to see that they did the best they could in the circumstances, and then see that it may not have been what we needed. Then we can sense what we missed, how we felt and allow ourselves the natural grief and anger that we did not have our needs met, resulting in a low opinion of ourselves and the belief that they did not love us - of course they did, they were doing the best they knew how. Worry and fear really influence people's ability to parent their children satisfactorily, even if the fear is coming from a belief within rather than an outside threat. When we are worried we fail to listen to what others need, a short term threat overrides the long term need of a child to receive adequate creative attention on a daily basis. Over a long period this damages the child's ability to communicate his needs and belief that his opinion or presence in the world matters. A child knows when his presence in the world is welcome or just tolerated. The child who knows he was an accident feels intrusive and unwelcome. The child of parents who wished for a child of the opposite sex will go to extraordinary lengths to try to make up for his or her failure to be what parents wanted. As a child I was often called clumsy and I only recently realised that I am a very careful person compared with most people; but I was brought up in family of extremely careful people so I appeared clumsy to them. I noticed that I was suggesting that one of my children was messy and untidy, then a child from another family came to stay and despite her best endeavour was much messier than ALL of my children, and I realised the message to me. I know someone who comes from a quiet family and was always considered noisy and extroverted by them. She got pushed to take on roles in public which she was uncertain about because the label only worked within the family circle and in fact she feels under pressure because of their expectations of her.

BE A GOOD GIRL

It is interesting to listen to what family members say to one another. I listen to them on the bus and in queues. The use of threats to make children behave in a certain way is very common, and they are usually empty ... from " I'll kill you in a minute if you don't stop" or "I'll murder you" to "You'll be walking home if you don't sit down" and "No one will want to play with you if you cry". Threats of what other people will do, say or think without any consultation are very common. The child learns to be afraid in case any of these things do happen - part of him wants to believe that his parents tell the truth - and he learns to mistrust what he is told. The use of bribes if a child is "good" has a similar effect and I was recently discussing the effect this had on a child with a friend. Part of the problem is that the child usually has to guess what is expected of him (just what does being good mean and does everyone agree on a definition?) and is often a completely unreasonable expectation of a young child (like sitting still or quietly for a long period). If you were a well-behaved child at school and the teacher said you would all go for a walk in the park in the afternoon if you were good children you would have restrained yourself or finished your work or whatever was required. If you were brought up in a family where people generally meant what they said, you would see it as a worthwhile aim. How do you feel now when you realise that the teacher was going to take you all anyway and even the naughty children who didn't finish their work went too? Quite a lot of what we learn is built on premises of this sort and it can be upsetting to realise that there is not after all a causative effect as we believed - or were led to believe - between our actions and reward by others.

This belief about cause and effect is widespread in abusive relationships where one partner seems to have power over the other. A woman who is injured by her partner often believes that she must have done something "wrong" to make him beat her - even if she has been making sure that she does everything she thinks he wants because he's done it before. She may spend ages trying to work out what it was so that she can feel he is justified and she's not living with an unreasonable man. Relationships are based on our experiences of them so far in our lives.

So how would a child be if it did get all those things it needed? Think about what your life would be like.

Being Really Helpful...
is providing what each child needs. This takes some careful consideration and enormous self control if you are trying to change habits in a family that has interfered unhelpfully.
First of all, listen. The child will probably be asking for what they need, if it isn't clear, clarify. "How would you like me to help?" Cope with the impatient answer, it will obvious to them! We are the grown-ups remember?

... 7 ...

PARENTAL LOVE

CHILDREN'S NEED FOR LOVE IS NOT BASED ON THEIR PARENTS' ABILITY TO GIVE IT

Parents love their children. The children may or may not recognise this. The attention we receive from them may not appear to be loving at all. It will be based on their past experience - and then the emotions are logical. Experience is stored for later use - the conclusion being the information we act upon. So, if, for example, a baby is born to a mother who is afraid of labour and whose last baby died, her justifiable fear may make her new baby conclude that life is frightening. With that amount of fear being around in your life even before you are born, you'd be right. Then there are plenty of things in the world outside to confirm the baby's opinion and nothing in the medicalisation of Western birth practices (including removing the baby from its mother just at a time when it needs reassurance most of all - and may conclude that she's died) to change it. Maybe a way to look at this is to see that this has been the baby's opinion of life so far - based on its mother's, but that this does not mean that life is always frightening; or that not everyone's life is frightening. I believe fear comes from a lack of fundamental support and readiness to move on to the next stage of maturity. Unfortunately it is so rare here in Britain to see a child completely confident that he will not be let down, that adults believe that children will not move on to the next stage of development unless pushed. Our experience of new experiences is therefore often tainted with having to attempt them before we are really ready and sure we can do something, and eventually afraid of failing - partly because adults also have a habit of laughing at their own children's' failures (there are reasons for this too) which makes the children dread trying the things their parents wish them to do so much.

After all this it is hard to remember how much the child needs the parent's approval. Children do want to please their parents and need to feel loved. Children's need for love is not based on their parents' ability to give it. Explaining this helps the intellect but does not ease the hurt of the child within (although it may help it to feel its hurt is justified). We need an appropriate way to express the many years of stored hurt. The Rebirthing process offers this - with a Practitioner who offers loving, emotional, non-judgmental attention. Our parent's parenting is often a reaction to the way that they were brought up - we may conclude that we are personally at fault for the harsh treatment (in our view) that we receive. Talk about it! You may find that it all makes sense viewed from their perspective: their parents were much stricter and they were being really relaxed (letting you stay out 'til 9.30 when you were 16 and really embarrassed because your friends had to be home at 11 o'clock, and your Dad thought he was being relaxed because he had had to come in at 8).

> 'Our children are our gurus, they teach us what we need to learn. Their punishment if they fail, is to grow up to be like us.'
> Leonard Orr founder of Rebirthing Breathwork in California, USA.

... 8 ...

WHAT RELATIONSHIPS ARE FOR

YOUR TASK IS NOT TO SEEK FOR LOVE, BUT
MERELY TO SEEK AND FIND ALL OF THE
BARRIERS WITHIN YOURSELF, THAT YOU
HAVE BUILT AGAINST IT

Sent to me by my friend Jo Tait.

We aim in our relationships to find satisfaction in communication, success that may have eluded us so far in our lives beginning in our families and developing through often superficial acquaintanceships, leading us to yearn for closeness in a personal relationship which we are probably not equipped to accept or recognise. The portrayal of love in our society is not based on an adult to adult relationship. The ideal of Romantic Love has been held up to be an attainable and desirable form of relationship between mortals; but when we look at it carefully and see what it entails we may see that we have been sold a pig in a poke. It is not what we have believed.

One careful listen to many love songs will demonstrate what it really involves (see "Romantic Love") and show how impractical and ultimately undesirable it is.

```
┌─────────────────────────────────────┐
│                                       │
│            ROMANTIC LOVE              │
│                                       │
│            Dependency                 │
│          Unattainability              │
│              Worship                  │
│            Possession                 │
│             Sacrifice                 │
│             Obsession                 │
│             Perfection                │
│           Helplessness                │
│             Salvation                 │
│            Exclusivity                │
│                                       │
└─────────────────────────────────────┘
```

These words might describe the sort of relationship between a mother and baby when the baby is very young, and the reason that we still seek it may be because that relationship was not fulfilled for us the first time around. Since it is rare for a baby to have those needs met it would follow that they still remain, even into adulthood. It is interesting that they are condoned in adulthood when they are frowned upon in childhood when they are appropriate. The feeling that "I will die without you (and your love)" is true in babyhood- a baby will die if it is not fed and cared for; the feeling that "you are the only one" is true too -you only have one mother. The words in songs describe this: "I'm not scared anymore, I'm not scared in the dark anymore when I sleep with you. You make me feel just like a child again … " The widespread use of the word 'baby' to describe a lover, male or female, shows the role of lover as parent. However, we do still have a need for someone who cares about us as adults, we have a need for friends, companions, family and in particular, for someone we are special to - a lover, partner, someone who has an investment in our happiness. However, in a mature adult this is not overwhelming, nor is the lack of a partner life-threatening. The characteristic of an adult relationship is that you can choose to remain in it, because the alternative of a solitary existence is acceptable. There are times when we need to be looked after when we are adult too: when we are sad, ill, have just had a baby … it is appropriate to ask for and to receive assistance and comfort at these times. This is not the same as needing someone to run areas of your life for you all the time or feeling that you can't exist without them. An inner knowledge of the fact that we could manage, but it's much nicer to do things with someone else, shows that we can balance our lives and meet our needs.

Why do we do this? I have a feeling that it is because we copy the style of relationship that we see: our parents' relationship is the most influential. Sometimes the details are different but the outcome is the same.

Choosing someone dependent as a partner because we are afraid of living alone is very popular.

... 9 ...
FEAR

IN EVERY LIFE YOU HAVE SOME TROUBLE;
WHEN YOU WORRY YOU MAKE IT DOUBLE.
DON'T WORRY, BE HAPPY
Bobby McFerrin

I have been investigating the source of fear because I
have come to the conclusion that it is a made-up
experience without a useful function. It appears to me
that it originates from the time that we discovered that
our mother was afraid and unable to be there for us.
There are useful states of caution, wariness, hesitation
but the problem with fear is that it blots out our
rationality and paralyses us. I remember a discussion
with my mother about teaching my daughter respect
and caution for the traffic on the busy main road where
we lived. I explained how it had taken me years to be
confident about making a sensible decision to cross
because I was afraid of the danger I felt I was in, and
how it caused panic - which was not at all helpful in the
position I was in - trying to safely cross the road. My
mother said she should be frightened to make her more
careful - I disagree with the fear element. And it is
interesting that I am less afraid than my mother and my
daughter is less afraid than I. It makes her more careful,
because she can see the danger objectively, and gives

her the ability to know her capabilities.

> Fear produces reactive behaviour and prevents independent thought. Obedience is therefore not a way forward for independent development.

It is also an advantage to have children whom I know can judge what they are capable of for themselves. My belief is that a baby expects its mother to be powerful and knowledgeable and to feel safe in the world. This is rare in our society; and especially rare at the time of childbirth.

... 10 ...

LIVING IN THE PRESENT

THE POINT OF POWER IS IN THE PRESENT MOMENT

The antidote to living in fear, with nervousness about what might happen, is to live in the present. At the present moment I am always beginning the rest of my life with the opportunity to change what has happened before if I want to enough. To do this I need to learn that I create what happens by the decisions I make. Life is a two-way process of interaction, so I need to learn that I have power. I also need to be willing to change; the way things have always been done feels secure but it may not suit me. I need to find other people to help me with this. I need to reassure my Inner Child that I will take care of her even though she is unhappy about me trying out new ideas. I can do this while I am afraid, and by doing so become less afraid. Once I have begun life with a new attitude I will find that life is on my side and helpful things will happen to encourage me. By making a statement and being committed to moving forward I will find that it is already happening. By being open I am allowing new possibilities to emerge. I may need to talk to myself encouragingly, to answer the critical voice which reminds me of the mistakes I have made before: "I know I chose the wrong way last time but I've learned and I'm not the same person as I was then, and that mistake has been a lesson and shown me what I don't want". For suggestions and the use of the technique of affirmation see books by Sondra Ray e.g. 'I Deserve Love' and Louise Hay 'You Can Heal Your Life'.

... 11 ...
ASKING QUESTIONS

As we relearn to breathe, we become aware of our feelings and our own opinions - sometimes for the first time in our lives. We find that as we have the confidence to consider change we begin to question the way that things have been, we begin to formulate the way that we would like things to be and then to plan how to go about achieving this. It takes some time, but along the way we may have flashes of sudden understanding which catch us by surprise and also lead to changes we would never have considered possible. One of the strengths of Rebirthing is that it helps us to see situations without judgement; when we no longer have an emotional investment in the way things turn out we are free to try new ways of tackling old problems. For example if we would like to be vegetarian, but are worried about the difficulties it may cause and embarrassed about asking people to provide meat-free dishes when we visit, we may find that once we trust ourselves that it is the right thing for us to do, lots of people enjoy the challenge of making Vegetarian meals, like the excuse for doing something they've been meaning to for ages and enjoy the discussion it provokes. We may find the most unexpected encouragement, and also respect - coming from others because we have begun to respect ourselves.

> A mother of grown-up daughters told me recently that when young her children would say: 'What are you really angry about Mum? what we did wasn't bad enough to make you that angry, Who are you really angry with?'
> She described herself as having a tantrum.

Once we have begun to challenge personal beliefs, we find that we don't accept things just because they've always been that way anymore. We may challenge family beliefs (I am the clumsy one), society's beliefs (It's unnatural for a woman not to want children; The man ought to be the breadwinner; It's not alright to be single and satisfied) and even cultural beliefs: this last one takes a lot of courage - challenging the inevitable (Everyone has to die; Fire always burns; Old people always get sick and helpless; We are the only sentient beings in the Universe). It's interesting that you will find that somewhere in the world these things are not assumed.

I would like to state here that just because we are questioning something (or indeed beginning to question everything), we do not need to change it. It is good to look at what we are choosing to do and to see it as that - a choice. It may look from the outside like what we have always done, but if we are choosing now to do something we felt obliged to do before, it feels completely different on the inside. How we feel about what we're doing is important, whether we are being true to ourselves, our beliefs and satisfied that it is a worthy way to lead our lives.

Freeing ourselves from traditional ideas can be so liberating. Just questioning the idea say, of physical death at roughly the same age as our parents (it's so common that insurance companies bet on it by basing their premiums on the assumption) - can mean that we feel that there is all the time in our lives to do all the things we really want to. I remember the feeling I had when I first entertained the idea(reading 'Physical Immortality' by Leonard Orr) a mixture of excitement and enormous relief/relaxation; I needn't rush anymore. There is plenty of time to do all the things I want to do. And sure enough, when I had taken up this idea, I read that medical doctors say that the human body is designed to last for 150 years. Well, that'll do for a start while I work out what I really plan to do ... It really doesn't matter whether we live for an astonishing length of time by western standards or not; once the idea is mooted, we have gained from entertaining the idea. Then, as Leonard Orr says, we'd better stick around and see if it is true ...

... 12 ...

RESPONSIBILITY

DRAW WHAT YOU SEE, NOT WHAT YOU THINK
YOU SEE
Bob Roper, my Art Master.

Funny word this; in current use it often suggests fault ("such and such a group has claimed responsibility for ... " - should we say irresponsibility in this case?) It means having the ability to respond. We live in a society which supports the belief that what happens to us influences the way we lead our lives, but not that the way we lead our lives influences what happens to us.

> Resist the temptation to tease. Think hard about how it felt when you were young, to be teased, not to know what the truth was, not to know what was happening.
>
> The time teasing is fun is when you both know what the truth is and you are playing. I read a good definition of teasing as something that both parties enjoyed, and if it became unpleasant for one party then it stopped. If it didn't then it was bullying.

The most we can expect if our faith supports the notion is that "our reward may be in heaven" - not now.

The truth is that everything we do has a consequence or a payoff, and we do things for what we believe will be the results we need. The difference between those of us who feel we are being genuinely selfless and those who know they get a kick out of it is that the second lot are aware of it! The next thing we have to deal with, is that if we are in charge of our lives (and responsible for ourselves) that means things we're responsible for altering things that we don't like, as well as taking credit for the things that work in our lives.

So we realise that we have the power to change. We are responsible for our relationships with those around us. There is no opportunity to blame any longer as we are responsible for our own reactions and feelings in all situations (including being gentle with ourselves while we still leap to blame someone who has 'hurt' us ...) and there is no place for guilt. Remember everyone always does their best. Guilt appears to be judging the way we are leading our lives by someone else's standards - when our own are perfectly good in their own right and more appropriate to our wishes in our lives. (The Inner Critic doesn't share our ideas or tastes and will always point out how we could have done something differently, that's its job and we don't need to act on any of its advice we don't agree with upon consideration, or feel bad if we don't.)

Since we are responsible for everything that happens to us, on some level we have made a decision, we are therefore able to aim for what we consciously want. On the way we will turn up all the beliefs that, perhaps unconsciously, have been directing our experience so far. We often let these slip in the way we speak, the phrases and generalisations that we use; "I always forget things", "I never get it right", "I'm stupid"…"Life's not fair", "Men are all the same" etc. I have become wary of using the words 'always' and 'never' as I have found that soon afterwards follows the exception to the rule. We also give away our dissatisfaction with life, which you may remember is of our own creation - what we expect to see, by complaining about, for instance, the weather: "how awful the rain is" is the one which stays with me. So many people complain, and yet we are so blessed to live in a climate in Britain where our food grows so successfully, that we have taken it for granted. I accept that there are some people who don't have a warm dry home to go back to, but those are not the folk I mean here. We can change our point of view and enjoy things we used not to like, I was going to say tolerate then but into my mind popped the example of me a few years ago plucking up the courage to face living on my own, I was steeling myself for a time of loneliness and responsibility that I would find a burden; I had no idea that I would enjoy it. The challenges that we dread most can sometimes not be as hard as we picture them.

This all means that there are no accidents and no random coincidences - no escape from responsibility, but at the same time we are in charge and in control of how much we choose to take on.

... 13 ...

CREATING OUR OWN REALITY

ENLIGHTENMENT IS THE CERTAIN
KNOWLEDGE OF ABSOLUTE TRUTH:
THE ABSOLUTE TRUTH IS THAT
THOUGHT IS CREATIVE
Leonard Orr, Founder of Rebirthing

Whether we are aware of it or not we are constantly creating our surroundings: the type of relationships we have, the amount of material wealth, our level of internal satisfaction - all are results of our internal expectations, our beliefs of what to expect from life. These are based on what we believe, what we think we deserve, our previous experience and the teaching of our parents, family and culture.

This truth helps to explain the different ideas taken for granted within families, which may in fact be remarkably inconsistent when put under scrutiny. We are brought up with "This is what happens, this is the way the world works" and so we see that which we have been shown. The brain likes to collect ideas together so we search out from our experiences things which make sense to us and 'Prove the Rule'.

> Expect them to copy you
> They need, and we are, role models, and they will use us and anyone around them: you may have to modify your behaviour. Some adults say that their children are getting undesirable habits from others, we are responsible for our part...it may be a useful spur to think what they may think of us as adults later but I would contend that it is unlikely that we can ever know what they think until they tell us later.
> We can only do our best. From observation those very habits we complain about them getting from others are more likely to be from us. It's just harder for us to see and admit this.

It takes quite a jolt for us to look critically at what we have been taught, and often we don't until we find it doesn't work for us, we feel unwell and unhappy and we want something more from life. There has been a slight cultural shift in that it has become acceptable for people to expect an improved quality of life (e.g. the increase in the divorce rate may not mean that marriages are no longer working as we may suppose that they were, merely that people are asking for more - seeing that there may be something better) and so more people are allowing themselves the choice of looking.

Be aware of the pitfalls - traps that you create for yourself to fall into - habits of attracting a certain type of partner for example, that you have experience of being unsuitable. Catch yourself before blundering into a similar situation again. Steer clear of potential trouble. Learn to recognise the warning signs.

Once we see what we would like to change, and what our beliefs so far have been we can change the programme. This takes acceptance of where we are - the current belief, why we needed it, forgiveness of ourselves for any mistake we seem to have made, and a thorough outline of what we now choose. What to do to change your reality: change your thought ...

1.   Awareness of current belief (this is covered in the next chapter).
2.   A 'shopping list' for what we now choose.
3.   Affirmations to assure us that we can do it - a response column to find our resistances (see appendix).
4.   "Cutting the ties" process if the change involves separation from someone we depend on for our image of self and forgiving them (see bibliography).
5.   Circular breathing at any time of stress in the process.
6.   Acknowledgement of ourselves as powerful beings able to create changes.

Because of the fashions of child-rearing in the recent past, the best way to feed your baby (and perhaps form its character by whatever method chosen) became an issue decided by the expert of the day. The reality for many adults today is that eating is not associated with simple pleasure; it has become complicated by our beliefs and past experiences. This is an example of how our past creates our present reality. (People worry about eating too much, being greedy or selfish, they believe they will have to pay for their enjoyment one way (getting fat?) or another. They forget that we eat to live and we are in a state of abundance.)

... 14 ...

AWARENESS

THE TIME IS NOW. THE PLACE IS HERE Dan Millman, 'The Way of the Peaceful Warrior'

The key to change lies in being aware of what it is we are already doing. The first step after you have been Rebirthing yourself for a while is to regularly become aware of your breathing. I found that the first thing I learned to notice was when I had stopped breathing momentarily, then I could remind myself gently to begin again, and give a thought to the situation that had made me stop in the first place.* This is so important because it is the key to movement, as we recognise and accept the situations that we have learned to avoid over the years. It is called suppression and it is a sort of denial; a pretence that any situation that we find intolerable doesn't really exist, so that we can live in familiarity or security - whatever it is that is so important that we choose to lie to ourselves rather than face an uncomfortable reality that is different to the scenario we have in mind. If we continue to breathe through any threats or dangers that we may perceive, we are able to see and accept each situation as it really is. This gives us a number of advantages:

We are dealing with only the situation in hand, not what

may happen if...

We can concentrate on one thing at a time;

Our minds are free to think of alternative outcomes to each situation, the right thing to say there and then - not later with regret;

We can delay the need to make a decision (which gives us time to think);

We don't antagonise people by being more aggressive/defensive than necessary because we are worried about the outcome;

We are receptive to the other people around us;

We sense their fears;

We realise that they mind what we think of them too ...

A way to practise being aware is to note what you can feel, see, hear, taste, smell as you do something. That brings me smartly into the present as I type this; I find that there is always something to rejoice about now, in the present, where I am, and this after all is I think what life is all about.

We have to know where we are starting from if we wish to journey anywhere.

If we become aware of something that we don't like and wish to stop the first step is to recognise we are doing it, the second to love ourselves anyway.

Hypocrisy is a puzzle to children. Part of growing up is trying to make sense of the world - seeking consistency. We, as adults, may not realise the things that we do are the very same things that we get so hot under the collar about if they do them.

Sometimes it is deliberate, I know, and some adults do want their children to seem better behaved than they, the parents, are. That's fine if you want a show, they will learn to do this. If you can see a particular time when this is a problem and you openly wish for dualistic behaviour, children will oblige if they can see the point and you may get their cooperation if they understand that it is a special case ("We don't use those words in front of granny, it upsets her").

Discussing it with the children really does help, and sometimes ends with surprising results. One way I found to remedy this was to ask for the children to help me by pointing out the things that I did that I did not want them to do. If you can't take it on the chin, I suggest you don't try this one: it works, but it hurts!

Only when we love ourselves as we are now do we lose the need for those addictive behaviours that we use to make ourselves feel better when we, and life, are not OK.

*By stopping breathing we are avoiding feeling things that we believe are horrid. Feelings that we don't like to own up to feeling, situations that we have been taught to avoid, and especially to express or show to others.

We have been taught that happiness is alright to express and sadness is not, some feelings are bad - even to feel, so we sometimes end up convincing ourselves that we really don't care about something. We may need to relearn that crying is a useful, wholesome and satisfying thing to do when the necessity arises; that disappointment is a natural feeling after certain occurrences from time to time; that grief is appropriate to a change in circumstances and perceived loss. Feelings have their own natural timespan and they are a part of our lives. Expressing them sends them on their way and lightens our load.

How do we recognise the Vague Paradise that will be the end of our searchings for happiness? We cannot expect any more than to be aware - true happiness is to be in the moment, and satisfied; "Whatever happens is perfect". Nobody said it was to get all we ever wanted, and absolute security is there for the taking. We choose to die when we are ready (although no one can guarantee what happens to us after death …), when we are tired of trying to work out the riddle. Even when we touch upon it, it tends to slip away again. What are we here for? To be unreasonably happy on the way; that's it.* Remember the goal is the way, not the end. When we are on the way we are living in balance. That does not mean everything works out happily ever after - or perhaps that's what the fairytales were implying: that once on the way, we follow the path - not that there would be no challenges. That would be dreadful! My daughter once said that this is Heaven; because if Heaven were as some people had suggested to her, it would be boring and not her idea of heaven - a decent heaven would come complete with challenges; so, this is it.

*Since the first edition I have read and reread 'Conversations with God' by Neale Donald Walsch. In his work the reason for being here is to find out and become Who We Really re.

Awareness in the newborn is acute, and throughout childhood it is generally acknowledged as superior to adult awareness. Sometimes my children gave signs of extra knowledge. I know that a parent scoffing at a gift a child has will make them keep it secret from then on, so we have no way of knowing how widespread these gifts are. When my son woke up one morning and came to me in bed, he said "Mum you know the coloured light you see around people, what do the colours mean?", I had a job to keep my composure because of my surprise and because I didn't have an answer when clearly he thought I would! So I told him I wasn't sure, we'd go to the library and find out. It took me a while to realise that one of my daughters had a gift for predicting the weather when she was about 2. We would ride into town on my bike and I would go outside before we set off and have a look at the sky to decide whether we needed to take a raincoat. One day she said quite certainly, that we didn't need to take a coat it would be fine all day. At first I didn't really believe her, then I realised that I could trust her, and needn't carry my coat!

... 15 ...

WHAT HAPPENS AT THE END
OF 10 SESSIONS?

What Rebirthing means to your life now

When you have learned the technique, you can use it at any time to accept and handle any situation in which you may find yourself. This may sound blasé or easy but it may not be - it is possible. By connecting the breath in the way we are designed to when we need to concentrate, we are maximising our presence in any situation. So we handle a difficult situation to our best, and we remember what to do next time; and we enjoy blissful moments to the full, allowing ourselves to feel all over our sense of joy. The other way you can use Rebirthing is to set aside a time when you will lie down for about an hour connecting your breath and allowing any vision, idea or memory to surface from your subconscious to your conscious mind for consideration. I have lots of new ideas for business opportunities, designs for paintings, clothes etc. by doing this, as well as a time to catch up to the present, assimilating all that has been happening in my life recently. Once open to change, we continue to release past stress and trauma when we feel ready and safe enough to do so. It is an on-going process. As time goes on more and more of my (self rebirths) breathing sessions are blissful experiences. It can be an extremely enjoyable and pleasurable process.

How life will change:

You will find that you have power in your life.

You will become more intuitive, and be able to get closer to people without being afraid of losing your sense of identity.

You will be aware of how other people feel and be more understanding.

You will probably wish to continue pursuing new ways of living your life, maybe making changes to your job, where you live, whom you live with. Whenever you stop or slow down your breathing you will become aware as you do it, so that you will be able at once to correct it and to investigate what it is that is disturbing you. Once you are aware you can then take appropriate action.

You will be able to tell people how you feel.

You will need to remind yourself that everything is going as it should, that if you trust and are certain about what you want, it will come. The reasons for certain occurrences may not always be immediately apparent.

Support for Change

As you change, the people around you will have a different relationship with you. Some people will like it, some people won't. You will attract new people into your life and some will not be a part of it anymore. Many Rebirthers run support groups for their clients so that there is somewhere that you know you will be able to share your feelings that you have learned to express and not everyone around you will be ready to hear. It is important to have moral support when altering the habits of a lifetime with a vested interest in keeping the status quo. (One of the main reasons we keep habits that do not serve us is because we are more frightened of change.)

... 16 ...

CONCLUDING ...

The magical element to life is that we can have anything that we choose ... because we have already created everything that we have.

By re-learning to breathe in the way that we were designed to do at birth in an atmosphere of love and safety, we can move on through trust to a more enlightened existence. That's what I knew was there as a child and searched for in the faces of the adults around me. I am delighted to say that I have kept some of the joys that I felt as a child, and lost a lot of the fears, and I have found some of the travelling companions I was searching for to share this extraordinary journey we call life.

THE PURPOSE OF LIFE MAY BE TO HAVE A GOOD LAUGH AND A CUDDLE

BACK TO THE BEGINNING

This chapter began life as an idea for a book called 'The Independent Baby - Reflections of a rebirthing mother'. I wanted to record the factors that I felt were significant and necessary to produce an emotionally mature independent adult. Once it was underway, I realised that these ideas tied in nicely with the new edition of Introduction to Rebirthing Breathwork that I was writing. I have therefore combined them in a form that I hope makes the connection clear, between the way we treat our children, and the adults that they become. We can use this information when we work as adults, to uncover the catalysts for our inadequacies, formed when we were children. It helps to know that there is a rational explanation when we struggle with our current inappropriate behaviour and endeavour to grow.

This is however, an opinion, based on personal experience and observation.

When I was training to be a breastfeeding counsellor, one of the questions that we were asked was "Which three things you would say to a mother who was on a moving train, as it was leaving the station, that would lead to successful breastfeeding?". As I write this, I wonder which three things I would suggest about raising children, like those given for breastfeeding.

I would venture to suggest these:
1. Listen to the child
2. Say 'Yes' whenever possible
3. Tell the truth, let them know who you are.

For further ideas on these and questions such as "How can a baby ask when it is too young to talk?", "How do I understand what they mean?", "What if I don't want to do it?" see my book 'The Reality of Breastfeeding' by Catherine Holland.

CREATING AN INDEPENDENT ADULT

I started thinking about how independent adults are created while I was writing my original introduction to Rebirthing breathwork. With the evidence of many of the adults I had worked with and the progress of my own children to observe, I concluded that the links are straightforward. This does not mean that it is easy to do, and I'm afraid to say that I failed sometimes to give my own children what they needed. Fortunately I didn't have to be perfect for them to turn out to be fine people! I hope too, that as I continue to grow, they have an example of the possibilities and choices that we all have. My knowledge and understanding of how we create our reality have grown. I have recently read 'Ask and it is Given' by Jerry and Esther Hicks, a further explanation for me of the way we attract our experience and how to be more deliberate about it. The most important understanding I gained from this book is the role of our emotions as a barometer for how closely we are following our dreams. If it feels good, do it. So I am dedicating myself to the excitement that I feel when creating. This is where the energy flows for me. I have tried to show my children, and my clients, that I practice what I preach.

The book was also instructive about the influences of others, however well they mean. Their wishes are not ours, their feelings are not ours. The way they go about things and what appeals to them are not ours. Tough, but true. So helpful remarks can be useful, but offers of solutions to problems have to feel right for me to follow them. Talking the problem through will often bring me ideas, and this is one of the ways that we can be most helpful to our children - by being a sounding board. I suppose that what I offer is a safe place, away from fear of ridicule for them to think aloud about their future, their ideas, solutions to work challenges. In this environment the part of us that explores can find an idea that will work. I can offer a trust that they will find a solution, possibly unsaid, but nevertheless important, when I consider some of the feedback offered by other adults. Many feel that there are no alternatives to those currently endured by people around them, usually working many hours at a job they enjoy little. The exception to this is the faintest hope that they will be saved by winning lots of money. This is alright if you really will feel happy doing nothing with money in the bank, but I feel good when I am pursuing some creative project, planning a trip, travelling or some such thing. The absence of debt is not enough!

It may be helpful to point out what not to do as well as what to do, partly because they contrast, and also because you will get a feel for the intention behind my suggestions. I will give you a list of things to avoid as well as a list of useful things to do. This is not exhaustive, and you will find more of your own.

These are examples of the ways that parents treat their children, and if changes are made the consequences of this misguided treatment of children may be prevented.

There are many life experiences that mould us that we cannot avoid.

We may fondly imagine that none of these apply to us, and I doubt whether all of them apply to anyone, but they can be subtle. I have used bald terms to describe them. Families dress up their bullying tactics "Granny wouldn't like you wearing that short skirt and you wouldn't want to disappoint Granny, would you?". This isn't about granny's preference at all.

If you don't have children and never plan to, you are still included, your treatment of yourself and your partner will be dictated by your family patterns as you grew up until you take charge of it.

Some Things to Avoid

Bribing
Threatening
Making them 'agree' with us
Breaking promises
Being hypocritical
Lying
Making a point
Making remarks
Unfair comparison
Letting them down
Asking them to do things we are not prepared to do ourselves
Tantalising
Teasing

Poking fun
Belittling their plans
Preventing disappointment
Forcing them into things
Controlling them
Trying to make them jealous
Crowing over them
Competing with them
Keeping them in the dark (perhaps literally as well as metaphorically)
Teaching them a lesson

Some of the above are expanded here:

Bribing
Threatening
Making them 'agree' with us - that is, making them lie

These may result in a child feeling obliged to allow something that they really disagree with; leading to an expectation of repeat behaviour by others who come to believe that they are willing participants. When this is done repeatedly, I believe that the long-term consequences will include depression, due to suppressed anger. This is the result of a betrayal of trust for the child, who has no choice but to concede to the adults around them.
Some adults do not realise the power of their size and, in men particularly, the volume of their voice.

Breaking promises

With children intent is not enough, they learn what we actually carry out, what they experience. Hurting them repeatedly, even if we say sorry, teaches them that we hurt them. Intention is no use to them unless it is backed up with action. This is especially true of young children.

> "The damage is done"
> "I blame the parents"!
> Two of my daughter's catch phrases.

Being hypocritical

Children spend quite a bit of their time trying to make sense of the world of adults, finding patterns so that they can predict what to do and stay out of trouble. Arbitrary behaviour unsettles them and causes withdrawal of trust to a greater or lesser degree depending on the behaviour and how honest we, as adults, are about it.

We adults may be uncomfortable with children expressing emotions that we have not come to terms with and may stifle them (the children) to save ourselves from confronting those issues.

We give leading and misleading examples.

Do as I say not as I do

Patterns are copied unconsciously, the examples we are giving are unconscious: the deliberate things that we do (to show them how to live) are a tiny portion of the fabric of their lives.

Suspicion is closely related to this need to create an impression in adults. It can only occur if we fear that we have something to lose and a feeling of distrust. Feeling that we are unworthy, any criticism is a "slur upon our character", our fears are probably true, we wouldn't be worried unless there were some foundation for them. For example, if someone gets upset when you disagree with them and says "Are you calling me a liar?" the chances are that they do tell lies. What I find strange is that telling the truth about them seems to be the worst thing that they fear. A child will become suspicious if it has been kept ignorant about decisions that affect him, and parents have been deceitful.

Lying

Parents may lie to their children to save themselves explaining an inconvenient truth. For example my neighbour used to tell her son the biscuit tin was empty to stop him from asking for more biscuits. He then saw her taking biscuits from the tin and knew that he had been lied to. This scenario was repeated in different areas of his life. He was lied to to control his behaviour. One day his harassed mother appeared at my gate and beseeched me "What can I do to stop him lying?".

My mother described to me how she had addressed this issue. She observed the pressure that children are under to please the adults who care for them. She said that she never backed us into a corner where we would have to lie.

The problem I see with adults who have been lied to is that they can trust no one. And sadly I can see no way to change this. They assume that everyone is lying.

If we examine the effect of lying, teasing and goading children once they reach adulthood - we find that they are distrustful and insecure. Trust is based upon kindness, fairness and expecting people to treat us as we have treated them. It is no wonder then that some children are rude to their parents.

NATURE DOES NOT PROGRAMME FOR PARENTAL FAILURE
Joseph Chiltern Pearce. 'Magical Child'

Making remarks

"Is that all you are going to eat?"
"Are you going out dressed like that?"
I would like to talk for a moment about eating here. Children will eat what is good for them if it is available. They will not eat food that is not available. Therefore it is up to us as parents to decide what to offer our children and then to say very little. We eat what we like, we cannot expect them to eat healthily if we don't.

They will always want to eat what we eat, or at least to try it. That's natural, it's what young animals do. So much damage is done by making food a big issue. The best thing that we can do is to treat it as fuel, a pleasure, and something we have our own preferences about.

Approval and disapproval lead individuals to change their behaviour. Trying to please us as parents and adults is natural to children who rely on us for their care. If we constantly comment on the way they do things; what they eat, what they wear, how they have their hair, they may not feel at liberty to express themselves. This can have serious consequences, producing among other things rebellious behaviour, simply because it is so important for each of us to be individual, rather than clones of our parents.

The judgement "Good boy" may as damaging as "Bad girl". What we are in fact saying to the child is something like: "You are only OK if you do what I like you doing". If you need to say something, may I suggest something like: "I'm really pleased with what you did today" - explaining exactly what it is that you are pleased with. The best example of the confusion produced by adults in this area is saying "Be good" and asking about a baby "Is she good?" without expanding this judgement. How does a child know what good means? It used to upset me when my babies were little. They woke frequently, fed frequently during the night, and in the end I could only cope emotionally by ignoring the comparison and judgement about babies, praising them for sleeping for long periods and seeking little attention. I enjoyed caring for them, and if they were awake and happy I loved their company. They can't help needing food and comfort, they aren't bad if they need to be cared for. This is also true later, as children are exhorted to be good, perhaps with threats if they don't. This is so unhelpful if the child doesn't have explained to them what is required of them and they are afraid of the threatened consequence, about which they then have no control.

Unfair comparison

Unfair comparison, indeed the need to compare at all, is not helpful. Sometimes comparisons are made as a result of transference eg suggesting that the other is putting on weight when it is themselves that has the weight problem; sometimes to try to get a child to behave more like another child, that the parent finds it easier to deal with. This is so unfair to a child who is only being itself, and after all is not fully developed, so they end up trying to develop their personality falsely. Shy children seem to be criticised in this way a great deal. Comparing them unfavourably with another child who is naturally more ebullient is going to undermine any progress the child is able to make about facing their fears.

Asking others to do things that we would not do ourselves

Creating false impressions

It serves to have a good memory of our own childhood and some humility, to be fair-minded in treating children with patience when they are uncertain. It would be alright to say "I don't like spiders, would you take that one outside please?". The problem is that an adult often does not want to admit to what they see as a weakness (being afraid of spiders). We each have different strengths, likes and dislikes. Children readily accept that adults need support and will happily help. Forcing them into the role without explanation is what I feel does damage. So it is not the act of asking someone to do something for you, it is the insinuation that they are somehow deficient if they don't do what you suggest - without any acknowledgement on the part of the adult that they find the errand nerve-racking. Where does such a strong need to impress come from that we see in so many adults? It leads to widespread attempts to cover up, deliberately creating (false) impressions. The only people who need to believe these impressions are the people trying to create them, after all!

Teasing
Poking fun

Honestly how well do you like it? When all is said and done teasing is lying. Some of the adults I know who do it, hate it if it's done to them and chastise children heatedly for lying.

It is a matter of discretion, while a child is finding a joke fun - and some children are masters at it - fine, but some children hate it and you can see this. If you care about them don't do it until they are ready. If you feel really strongly that they need to learn about it, don't just tease them, tell them.

Humiliation, felt by a child who is made to feel inferior by older people may become belligerent or apathetic as an adult, depending on how extreme the treatment is, and whether they have any other adult support. We may feel that what we subject the child to is perfectly acceptable, particularly if everyone else appears to be doing it, and no one objects. My experience of talking to adults who relive episodes of their childhood is that these incidents feature strongly and have a profound effect.

Which things really matter?

Some people argue that children can cope. Adults have said to me: "They know when I'm joking". This may be true, I would suggest that this depends on how often, what subject is under discussion and the age and understanding of the child - that look of bewilderment on the face of a child struggling to understand distresses me as they may be humiliated. Adults frequently recall these incidents during personal growth processes as fundamental to the destruction of their self image.

Belittling their plans

Absence of this can mean that a child succeeds in his chosen path. By this I mean to suggest that it is so common for children's plans to be ridiculed that their dreams are crushed even before they have formed. Those moments when a child says "I want to be a pilot when I grow up" have importance. Our reaction to their statement of their dreams is influential. Few people ever enter their chosen career. Most people end up doing a job they hate. Few aspire to the way of life that would make them happy. I believe that many more of us would be happily living our lives if we'd had the encouragement and trust of our parents and other adults around us. Every time we express doubt that a child would be able to carry something through, we remove some of their motivation.

When questioned about this belittling, a parent will say that they are just being realistic. So they doubt that their child will be able to achieve their dreams. If their parents don't support them, they never will.

If we belittle children they will be reluctant to express their plans, dreams and feelings to anyone.

Have you ever noticed how successful racing drivers are often a father/son team?

Preventing disappointment

This is a powerful motivator for a parent and a problem for their child. We need to try things out for ourselves. Our experience will not be the same as that of our parents. Indeed, what to them was a disappointment may be a success in our eyes. At least if we try something we have a chance of success, if we don't try we can never succeed.

Forcing them into things
Controlling them

Forcing children to see people, for example family throughout their childhood, puts them off for life. They then can't choose to see who they like and so may see none.

Drunken parents waking their children in the middle of the night wanting them to perform party tricks for drunken friends show their lack of consideration fuelled by their alcoholic misjudgment.

Forcing children is unthinkable to those brought up to listen to children - the foundations for teaching respect. Do not take advantage of their small size and apparent weakness. I remember appreciating my friend's patience, not rushing her little daughter. Sarah then said of Kathryn, 18 months: "She wouldn't let me". Sarah would not override Kathryn's objections, she listened with respect to her little daughter.

I was told when my children were young that

mismanaged toddlers turn into rebellious teenagers. I suspect that this was said because it is possible to force a small child to do what you want them to; parents find this temptation too much to resist. It comes home to roost later when the young adult reacts to having choices made for him. Respect is gained by demonstrating it. All this is laid down as the baby grows through childhood with whatever treatment we give him. It is important that he learns to make his own decisions by doing i. The decisions made by a toddler will affect his life in significant ways at that time, but making a wrong decision will be a safe lesson, when made in a protected environment. These decisions are very important in learning judgement and our experience of trusting our own judgement. Deprived of this early experience, young adults do extreme and dangerous things to test their boundaries.

WHY DO ADULTS THINK THAT THEY ARE STRONGER THAN CHILDREN?
Peter aged 4.

Trying to make them jealous
Crowing over them
Competing with them

Avoid constant competition - why would an adult need to compete with their own child? We are in a sad state of immaturity if we need to do such a thing. We can work on developing our internal parent to change this, allow ourselves to do things that we love that may seem pointless; buy a kaleidoscope, paint our toenails, have a swing …

Keeping children in the dark

"She should let us know what's happening", said in anger with abusive adjectives! By a 60-year old man about his landlady. Where did this originate? Is it current or does it tie into our upbringing when we were not given warning about important events and suitable explanations for things that would affect us. For example, a (divorced) parent moving house and not telling their children. The children found out by being taken to a new house when they next visited.

Teaching them a lesson

This suggests that we can set out to implant a particular set of thoughts into a child's mind. We cannot. They draw their own conclusions from their experiences.
Whatever grand ideas adults have about what is good for all children, like Truby King who believed that it would be good for babies to be taught to wait for their milk, we can only conjecture what they learned instead. The philosophy of teaching them (babies) to wait may have actually taught them "My mother doesn't care about me" or depending on their personality "I am unworthy", "Nobody likes me", "I am unlikeable", "No one hears me", "I am unimportant". At an early stage

babies are reactive, their opinions about themselves within their world are forming, they are very literal.

Any blanket guidance for children is going to create problems, as you will understand if you have read this far, for the simple reason that every child is different and needs individual attention to thrive.

EVERY CHILD NEEDS SOMEONE WHO IS CRAZY ABOUT THEM

John Holt author of 'How Children Fail' and 'Teach Your Own'

It is a puzzle to me that women are so ready to listen to childcare advisors, whose opinions come and go with fashion. Perhaps this is because our traditional infrastructure of family support has been eroded away, and they still need guidance from some authority. Mothering and childcare is something that humans are designed to learn by example, it is not wholly instinctive.

Teaching a lesson also suggests punishment. I think this comes from an immature need for retribution on the part of adults who have not been considerately treated when young. It is noticeably absent from emotionally mature individuals.

People do dreadful things when they are under unbearable pressure. The amount of pressure we can bear is a result of a combination of genetics, upbringing and situation - some people can do wonderful things in appalling situations (see Bruno Bettelheim 'A Good Enough Parent' a fascinating, but laboured account of child-rearing practices in America and the effects of them on teenage behaviour, also his slightly unorthodox procedures for dealing with their behaviour. Observations of similarities between people under unreasonable pressure and descriptions of acts of extraordinary generosity and altruism from his experience in a wartime concentration camp). It is not human nature to be destructive and unkind. We all have the capacity to be inspired with support. Growth is always an option.

Some Helpful Things We Can Do:

Listen
Foster their independence
Value their ideas and advice
Observe their need for freedom, acceptance, lack of criticism
Give them freedom to choose
Show them and answer them
Be a sounding board
Be genuinely interested
Massage them and ask them to massage us
Provide raw materials
Respect their privacy, possessions and their creativity
Let them see who we are, tell them what we like about them
Explain what is happening

Some of the above are expanded here:

Listen

The most important thing that we can do to tailor our parenting to our child's needs is to listen to his expression of those needs. When tiny, they will be clear if we are listening. We can try offering each comfort he may need in turn until we learn the subtle differences between his requests for each of his needs. It takes some days to get to know a new baby intimately.
We also need to listen to ourselves. The tone of our

voice can be very powerful, all the difference between appreciation and sarcasm, for example "What a surprise!" or "Thank you very much" (I have heard these said with sarcasm.)

Foster their independence

Assume that they do wish to be independent and that their efforts are directed at this outcome.
We often don't trust them to develop and in trying to force maturity, in fact prevent it …
Older children who have received the attention they need are happy to look after themselves and competent to look after younger siblings.
At the other end of the scale, once damaged, a child may take a very long time to be ready for independence. The damage done to some children means that they do not want to become adults. Children thrust with responsibility too early in their lives do not to wish to step into adult shoes. I was shocked to hear such a child say: " I don't want to be grown up".
This is rare. Generally they will be only too willing to attempt everything if we will allow them to.

Value their ideas and advice

Valuing their individuality, ideas and advice follows neatly on from the last point. Children have to be allowed to find other ways of doing things. If they have a new way of doing something that works equally as well as our old way, why shouldn't they do it their way? I believe that one reason that teenagers question the status quo is to ensure that new ideas are introduced into society. Sometimes their fresh way of looking at things can save us a lot of trouble!

This learning business is by no means one-way. It is sadly still not fashionable to listen to one's children for helpful ideas and advice. I don't know why. Such a lot has changed since the Victorian era, but not this. I was thrilled when my mother first telephoned me to ask for my advice about something, and my children are a wonderful source of inspiration.

What we think we are teaching children and what they are actually learning may be very different. How can several turn out so differently with the same parents? Their experience comes from a combination of personality and their position in the family.

They need us to be useful to them in their growth and development: to be open-minded (our culture has given us expectations) and ever-watchful of our own behaviour, to question everything but not to alter it for the sake of it, to listen to them when they point out our inconsistencies.

> I remember my father puffing and panting to move our upright piano around a much smaller piece of furniture. I tentatively suggested that he might move that around the piano instead. He took a moment, then the idea to sank in and he decided to do what I had suggested. I think it was an important moment for me, as I remember it so clearly. I guess I was about 7 at the time.

Show them and answer them

One of the hardest things for adults to do seems to be to answer a straightforward question with a straightforward answer.

We don't have to prove that we are smarter than they are: they are children.

Being the adult means being clear, setting boundaries. Once we become a parent we are always responsible for that standpoint. So, for example, if we have a disagreement that is serious enough for a difficulty in communication, I believe that the parent is the one who is ultimately responsible for re-opening communication if it has become difficult, a stalemate. It is possible that we have made a mistake, and it is alright to apologise and open the communication again.

Be a sounding board

Listen, say very little, let them talk until they see a suitable solution for themselves. Have no vested interest in any decision they make, so that they can choose clearly what works for them. When an adult wants the child to take their advice so that they can have a part in their success, the decision is no longer owned by the child, and is then clouded by a wish to please their parent. Get a life of your own, don't live vicariously through your children.

Be genuinely interested

Make sure you have support so that you are strong enough to do the job well.

Massage them and ask them to massage us

I was introduced to baby massage when I had my second child. It turned out to be a lovely time, my first child wanted to be included and then they wanted to massage me; a wonderful idea!

Provide raw materials

A child's fertile imagination will use whatever is at hand to create the extension of their imagination. My children spent hours with old wrapping paper, cornflake packets and paint. I invested in a small climbing frame and my daughter suggested building a sand pit and later a pond. She also collected large pieces of wood and a lorry towing chain, I don't know where she got that from. She proceeded to build all sorts of dens and a lookout for her little brother to stand on; he was too short to see out over the fence and too young to go out of the gate. I have heard parents making fun of their child's need to collect things. I feel that it is an important stage of their development.

When it is time to dismantle their creations, do so sensitively with their knowledge and involvement.

Respect their privacy, possessions and their creativity

I was brought up in a family where privacy was respected. I suspect that this was partly as a result of my parents seeing what trouble could brew up if we found out things that we weren't supposed to! Apart from the courtesy of treating our children in a way that we would like to be treated ourselves, if we poke our noses into their business we then have to deal with the consequences of knowledge that we gain and are then responsible for, as well as the fact that our children will become secretive.

I believe that watching them while they nervously do something new that they are uncertain about is a mistake, unless they specifically invite us.

Sometimes we will like what they do and sometimes we won't, but that is no reason to run them down.

Let them see who we are, tell them what we like about them

Express yourself. We need to show our children what is truly important to us, to let them know us.

Sharing what we are passionate about gives them an example to follow. Explaining what we believe and why, lets them form opinions. Saying that we don't know everything means that they can offer their own. Allowing our partners to share themselves with our children separately is important for them to see who we are too.

When they move from being adoring little children to critical young beings, we may have to stand our ground and explain that we don't run down their attempts and we'd appreciate it if they respected ours. It is rare for children who have been shown consideration to be challenging in this way, but they do have other influences and occasionally test us.

When we tell them what we like about them, we increase their self esteem, make them proud of who they are and encourage them to do their best.

Explain what is happening

Be considerate. We are training these children to be adults that we would like to be friends with.

We can describe what's happening in ways suitable to their level of understanding so that they know we are including them. This works for future plans as well as practical, day-to-day issues. A friend helped me to keep my toddler out of my walk-in pantry, where all my china was kept at a convenient level for her to reach, by suggesting that I explain to her while I removed her. I was puzzled by this because she wasn't yet able to talk, but sure enough it worked. Unceremoniously removing her produced a violent reaction, gently explaining why I didn't want her in there worked a treat. Needless to say this was a valuable lesson that I did not forget.

Another object lesson for me was the shedding of deciduous baby teeth. I thought this occurred when children were about 7-years-old, so I had plenty of time to warn my 5-year-old about this. She was absolutely distraught when 2 front teeth came out when she was playing with Lego. It took a while for her to calm down enough so that I could explain that she would grow new ones. I then set about warning her about everything that would happen as she grew up, giving her the chance to ask for explanation suited to her understanding at the time. This stood me in good stead because all my children knew about sex, reproduction and death while they were unemotive issues and they were merely curious. It brought a useful openness to our relationship that has been set for life.

It goes without saying that most parents discuss major events in detail to prepare their children for changes such as when they will be moving house; not all do however. Adults whose parents have kept them in the dark come to personal growth with issues of trust to be resolved.

OBSERVATIONS

Some common threads run through immaturity in adults. These seem to be the result of having been treated in ways that I suggest to avoid above, as they create insecurity and therefore immature behaviour.

I guess some parents and grandparents would be horrified to discover the effect that their apparent playing had had on their young charges; particularly teasing, as far as boys are concerned and particularly belittling, as far as girls are concerned. The children often try to hide their upset, partly to stop them being criticised for being over sensitive, and partly because they want to have the advantages of keeping company with these important adults. Some of these effects are unintentional. Beware, for example, of sending children to bed as a punishment, this can cause inability to enjoy going to bed as an adult.

Remember that we are individuals, so any comment on variation is damning. It doesn't have to be as strong as criticising, suggesting that being different is a sign of mental derangement is not uncommon. People worry that they are going mad if they wish to assert their individuality in some very normal ways, just because their family suggested that it was not alright to be different. Raising children is like rebirthing adults, everyone needs something different and everyone knows what they need, if we know how to listen. This explains why children raised in the same family can have such different experiences of the same parenting, as well as the different interaction between personalities.

Different children need different mothering and fathering, and with the child that asks for a lot it can be hard to sift out the important requests.

It may be helpful to describe the quality of attention a child needs. A baby does not need to be the centre of attention for most of the time. If he is, he can suffer from becoming the focus of the parents' life and too much is expected of him, because they are living vicariously through him.

Lack of respect for others naturally follows, particularly partners, taking the place in adulthood of family members, and thus becoming magnified in personal relationships. The balance that needs to be struck is for the baby to be attended to when he needs something and the parents to be otherwise engrossed in something that interests them.

Out of the mouths of babes

This well-known saying alludes to the fact that children make astute observations - and we laugh at them finding them cute or funny - but we often do not stop to follow their way of thinking to develop and foster it.

I recall my neighbour telling me that her daughter had taken to saying "I want AND need it" because her mother had said "You don't need it: you want it". Fortunately the mother was aware enough of her daughter's ability to judge her own needs to realise that she really could trust her to know what she needed for herself.

The meaning of cute incidentally comes from acute - sharp, we are sometimes unnerved by the brightness of children. Some adults try to hide their embarrassment at being shown up by the child, by ridiculing the child. This, unsurprisingly, is not explained to the child who is bewildered and concludes things from these experiences such as: "It is not OK to express my thoughts", or "I make people feel uncomfortable". This in turn affects their interaction with folk as they grow up. Perhaps it encourages shyness later? I have heard adults expressing an opinion that other people won't be interested in what they have to say. This is not a normal thought and must have been produced by some negative feedback.

Influence

No less than a flowering plant, a child's genetic programming is there for development, only different from a plant because of the child's complexity. Perhaps it is easier to thwart because the balance is more delicate; there are more variables to stick a spanner in the works. This may be a useful analogy. It is dramatic to see how plants are influenced in shape by their position. Take for example, the variation in height and shape of a tree, maybe an oak or a hawthorn. They have a clear outline if left to grow alone in the middle of a sheltered field, but exposed on the coastline or the on the moors in the harsh wind, they take on a profile as though constantly in the blast of a gale - shaped over to one side - and their growth is stunted, sometimes only a tenth of what it might be elsewhere. I like this analogy because it works with space too. Have you noticed how trees grow in a forest? If they are crowded together they are tall and narrow, wherever there is a gap they strike through it to gain some space and light. This may be how the forester likes them to grow, with few branches and a straight trunk, but is it best for the tree? What happens if those surrounding trees are removed? We saw something like this in Slovakia where there had been a tornado across the mountainside. Those trees that survived the initial blast later fell, as they were too weak to stand alone. Can you see parallels with human treatment and behaviour here?

I think certain institutions are formed so that people do not find themselves able to think independently. Sometimes it is deliberate and with consent, as in the armed forces where the system would collapse unless people worked together unquestioningly, as trained. Sometimes it is done with less willing participation, as in educational and religious establishments - especially for those too young to be aware of, and therefore unable to resist, the system.

Asking

We parents spend much of our time teaching our children to be polite to others. We teach them to treat us in a way that we find acceptable, and we teach them to treat others in a way that we feel is acceptable. Sometimes this is deliberate instruction, but more often it is not. They learn from the way that we treat them (the children) first of all, from the way that we treat others (their other parent, their siblings, other family members, the general public), and sometimes - even more invisibly perhaps - from the way that we treat ourselves. I have observed many differences in family etiquette and the extraordinary ability of children to learn different nuances in behaviour for different situations.

I found that the best way to deal with this while raising my children was to discuss this with them, once they reached the stage of wanting to understand why certain behaviour was appropriate with some people present, but not others. This does lead to the parent having to justify their own behaviour, and sometimes to rationalise it! But I found it a useful exercise.

Unbelievably, some children are punished for asking directly, politely, for what they need. It seems extraordinary that something as apparently simple as asking for what we want can cause such complication. What could be the possible advantage to a parent for not responding to a reasonable request on the part of their child?

It is logical, if not obvious, that by discouraging a child from asking for what it needs we are making it deceitful (teaching it to lie). If we punish them for telling the truth, they will say what they hope we want to hear, by trial and error, until they find out how we react most favourably to their requirement. There are needs that children have (adults too) that have to be met. If they cannot ask in a straightforward way, they will learn a method that brings them what they need. The child will try asking, crying, getting ill, shouting, whatever it takes to get the attention that they crave - any attention is better than being ignored. I suspect that this (ignoring) is one of the most powerful methods for influencing children, whether or not it is deliberate on the part of the parent. We come back again to the point that children learn from what they experience, not what we might set out to teach them.

Children ask in an open manner for what they need unless discouraged. This is reported by those who visit more isolated communities in various cultures: that the people are direct, they ask what they would like to know. There is nothing wrong with this (nor with answering "I don't want to tell you"!) unless we have been taught that there is.

It is wonderful if we can allow them to be different, not imagining that they are trying to change us, or ungrateful for our upbringing if they choose something different for themselves.

Yelling at them doesn't work

All it produces is insensitive people who do not react to quiet requests, so you spend your life shouting. It's a bit like the English speaking to foreigners more loudly in English when they don't understand … It must be their fault, there can't possibly be anything that we could do to change.
So we continue the theme of: if the children are doing it the chances are that they have learned it from us.

If you sincerely wish to alter the situation, ask yourself, do I ever do it? Do I do it in front of them? Do I wish to reprimand them for things that I do myself? This requires serious awareness and cooperation if you both wish to provide a united front. For example when teaching children to cross a busy road using the pelican crossing, during the influential years you must always do so yourself, if you sincerely wish them to do this even when you aren't there.
The other thing that this takes is trust, once they are ready to cross the road themselves, trusting that they will do so safely.

Helping

Adults often march in over a child's attempt to do something and show them how to do it. This has not necessarily been asked for, and may not be helpful at all. The child may have learned more by doing it themselves. Interestingly the tension produced in the adult witnessing a child's slow progress seems to be what prompts the interference, rather than any request on the child's part for help. And if they do ask, it is most helpful to check what exactly they wish you to do, it may be the small bit that they can't manage. Whether the child asked for the help or not it seems to get stored in the adult's compartment of "After all I've done for you" to be wheeled out at a later date during an argument!

Why are we doing what we do for them?

Clumsiness

Clumsiness seems to be a subtle signal of pressure that the person is under. I notice that before I am aware that a situation is troubling me, I start dropping things, particularly keys. I would venture to suggest that children appear clumsy when they are uneasy. I would also like to suggest that you don't watch them completing a task that they are unused to, to see if they make mistakes, that's really mean.

Worrying

This is a lack of trust that children will protect themselves and ensure that they get what they need. This is epitomised for me in the urging to "Take care". Surely they know enough to take care of themselves without us doing it for them? and I believe that these exhortations distract the child. Children are very resourceful. We live in a Nanny state where we expect others to take responsibility for our safety and actions, protecting us from ourselves. This is not how to make real grown-ups! Judging the right moment when a child is ready to make the step into independence is hard for us, but the clue is in the child. Listen and they will tell us.

Make sure that you think ahead and have something interesting and fulfilling to take the space that they used to fill, so that they can leave you, and not worry about you!

If you worry so much that children feel unable to pursue their own lives they will develop coping strategies, one of these is never to let you know what they are doing, where they are going and for how long they will be away, so that you cannot take them to task for letting them down. This is quite common, and leads to problems with unreliability in adulthood.

Unfortunately if we worry about them, our children learn not to trust their own judgement and that of others. They can even be convinced that it is a sign of caring, and that lack of worry means that we don't care about one another. If children have been convinced of this by their parents, the children have a hard job to disentangle this sort of legacy to produce clear connections in their adult lives. This sort of caring is used as a controlling mechanism. The child knows that it is being constrained but cannot free himself and never pursues his dreams.

> My 7-year-old daughter had insisted that I accompany her wherever she went throughout her childhood. One day she turned to me and said: "I'm going out and you're not coming with me". She spelled it out because she knew that I would be surprised. She never asked me to accompany her again.

Unfinished Business

We find echoes of babyhood in adult behaviour. Why do they remain? How can we avoid this in the next generation?

These anomalies are provoked by the care being insufficient for the baby's needs. This is most likely to have been caused by the parent not being equipped for parenthood by their poor upbringing. And so it goes on. One manifestation of baby behaviour in adulthood makes us identify too closely with our partner's behaviour. She isn't our mother, and isn't like her in every way, even though we may perceive this to be the case. It also makes us expect inappropriate care from another adult and resentful if they fail to provide this.

One of the signs is an inability to cope with small incidents. Each becomes a disaster, out of proportion in reaction and description: "There's water all over the floor!" (there are 6 drops of water) - perhaps seeking a reaction. This is the behaviour of an adult suffering from not receiving the right sort of attention as a child, and so seeking any attention. This is also where classic naughty boy syndrome begins. I believe that this is due to the fact that culturally we ignore many of the needs of boy babies to make them tough to live in "the real world". Thus they have a greater need for attention as it has not been fulfilled.

It is difficult to deal with these leftover behaviours in someone who is otherwise a competent adult. What should we do when we are with people who are being horrid? I read a useful little library book about being bullied to encourage myself to hold my ground in certain situations. It was from the children's library and had a useful suggestion to repeat silently to yourself that you are a fine person when someone is saying destructive things about you. Create something along the lines of "I am a fine person, I know I am OK".

Living in the present

Emotional maturity means not worrying about what might happen, a certain perspective - the ability to witness, acceptance, faith, trust that the Universe is a safe place. We occasionally meet children with this emotional maturity. Our full maturity in this regard is supposed to be complete by the time we are 7-years-old. This is only the case if we have received what we need. Many western adults have not and that's why they turn up asking for assistance and breathwork sessions.

Trust, acknowledging that there could be other outcomes than what we KNOW will happen from previous experience and seem inevitable, takes training and patience. There are a lot more possibilities of happening than we can predict.

If we train our children with kindness they will understand acceptance. Taking what comes in life is not giving in, giving way, being soft. It is dealing with what is really happening now.

How do we react when someone says "No" to something that we want? this is a good test of how accepting we are. Some people say "OK thank you for trying", some people try to persuade the other to agree, some react angrily.

Anger *directed into action* is healthy. Realising how we feel and acting on it appropriately at the time uses the feeling constructively, using the energy to precipitate change in our circumstances. Rebirthing Breathwork gives us the opportunity to work on issues from our past. Anger is frequently suppressed, springing up later with inappropriate vehemence. Working through this can identify the original cause and give outlet to the past feelings - bringing us into the present.

> Anna about 8-years-old:
> "I'm so angry I'm going to do the hoovering".

My daughter was explaining to me recently how she believes that being considerate is one of the foundations of a healthy adult relationship. It shows maturity on the part of each person, that they consider the other person's wishes as well as their own. This is shown in letting people know if we are going to be late, developing habits that fit in with the person we spend time with, discussing plans. It is a demonstration of personal power, that we accept responsibility for our actions. It is a pleasure to witness her interactions, showing her extraordinary communication ability as well as her maturity in choice of lover and friends.

Get support

All of this requires strength and dedication. We need support for ourselves as parents from somewhere. Finding suitable support is challenging since many of the things we are trying to do go against cultural norms. The first one is the support of your partner; discussion with them, with and without the children, is useful. Once the children reach the age where they can talk, they can help in decision-making, though I would suggest that they are included before this. Family can be wonderful support, but may not be the best people for helping you to develop new and different ways of parenting. I have found support from the childbirth and breastfeeding organisations truly wonderful (I made friends there for life), as well as in some unexpected places. La Leche League has a child-centred philosophy designed to treat children as individuals as well as helping with breastfeeding. I was not convinced that schooling was good for children, but if you are then the Rudolf Steiner and European schools scattered around the country are sympathetic to the individual child.

Relax, you don't need to know everything, you only need to be willing to support them while they learn.

HOLD HIS HAND ...

Of all the suggestions that I would make I think that this would be the most important: Hold his hand, first of all literally and then figuratively. See the world from his point of view. When we are little we need adults to support us and to help us negotiate, to teach us how to do this for ourselves. Our job as parents is to be sensitive to how long this is necessary for. Some children are clear about what they need and others are not. In that moment of hesitation on the part of the child, offer and ask. Be pleased when they refuse and are capable of making their own way. The difficulty I see many adults have in helping their children in this way, is that they insist that the child has to learn to fend for himself. In other words they don't want to help. I believe this situation arises because we have not been helped properly ourselves (the parents), which makes us afraid of approaching people when there is a problem to be dealt with, particularly with someone in authority.

One of the observations that I have made is that we treat boys and girls differently in this regard. Boys are offered less support, and while this means that they are less often prevented from trying things for themselves, it also breeds false confidence and a fear of asking for help. So many more young men get thrown into hedges from motorbikes and cars than young women, from failure to measure their ability and familiarity with their machine. Being expected to know things brings a fear of not knowing, and of others finding out that we don't know. It also brings courage to try things in case we find out that we can do them, a natural trial and error that brings success much of the time.

CONCLUDING THE SECOND EDITION

I didn't think that I was doing anything really special as I brought up my children. I knew that I was doing my best, and I knew that I worked hard at it, but I didn't realise how few other parents were doing the same thing. Coming into contact with adults in a setting where their experience of growing up became known to me in unusual depth, meant that I began to piece together some of the cause and effect of child-rearing practices. The adults I was working with were a product of their interpretation of their experience.

Reinterpretation of that experience can bring peace. Breathwork is a very efficient way to do this. As my friend who introduced me to it said: "It's drastic but it's quick!"

And if you have chosen to walk with me through these pages remember we are the teacher and the student: always proud and humble, proud of what we have achieved with the humility to listen to what our children (clients) have to teach us. It is a narrow path, to be able to switch from parent to student of those same children that we are raising. Harder still, in our adult relationships when we can see the needy child in our partner, and know that there is nothing that we can do to ease their suffering. As an adult it is now up to them.

ADDITIONS FOR THE THIRD EDITION

The maintenance of total health

In creating this 3rd edition with the new subtitle *The making of an independent adult*, I have had the opportunity to reflect more deeply on what creates health. Writing my recent book *Indestructible Soul: How I decided not to die*, gave me the chance to reflect on why I didn't die, what factors were key in making me so robust that I was able not only to withstand using half my blood in a few minutes, but to heal so well following this trauma in the next few weeks, and the following years, of recovery.

The body's ability to stay well depends on a number of predictable factors.

In the 8 years since this book was last published, I have been able to draw some conclusions about the wider use of breathwork and the implications of this. This also gives me the chance to observe what happens when we don't breathe fully and attend to our body's needs over time.

My conclusions are:

1 That the out-breath is as healing as the in-breath.

2 That food is either nutritious or toxic.

3 That our bodies are capable of keeping themselves well.

4 That by the time we notice symptoms of disease, trouble has been brewing for a long time.

1 It's as important to breathe out the build up of waste gases as it is to increase the amount of oxygen available, if not more so. This is often something outside our conscious control, and one of the reasons that Rebirthing Breathwork training has such a profound effect on our physical health.

2 What we consume in food, and more importantly water, contributes much to creating the environment of the body, for example how acid or alkaline it is, although it is secondary to breathing in creating this. It is becoming clear through study that certain common foods are in fact not nutritious, and are indeed toxic to the human body. This leaves the body with a huge job of having to excrete materials that are damaging while not receiving the nutrients it needs to do so.

3 Our bodies have an extraordinary capacity for adaptation, and they efficiently control homeostasis (keeping levels of important minerals, hormones, antibodies, circulating effortlessly). The state of flux in the body is akin to the contents of a flowing river, and this relies on enough of the correct nutrients as well as water, for the system to function correctly. And of course we are responsible for eating enough nutrient dense food and drinking water, just as we are for breathing fully.

4 It takes years, or decades of neglect for our bodies to get ill. We have to ignore its needs for a very long time

for it to be unable to right itself. It will bend over backwards to enable us to continue functioning, and has all sorts of clever ways to use different nutrients and methods to cover for what it perceives to be a shortage in our environment. It cannot however, cope with the long-term lack of supply of vital nutrients, which I have realised now come from uncooked food, that which has been heated to less than 45 degrees C or 117 degrees F, or lack of water. Strangely in our oversupplied Western world, and I speak as a British person, we are living in a perpetual state of drought within our bodies, for lack of water.

I have told you all this because the bringing of oxygen to the lungs is only the first stage of the supply of oxygen to every cell of the body. What happens to it once it has passed the membrane in the lungs, and been taken up by the haemoglobin in the red blood cells, is the next important stage of what happens to it on its journey to where we can effectively use it to maintain total health.

The way to correct this is described in my guide Indestructible Health which is short enough for me to include in full here. It is also available free as a 7 page eGuide from my website.

INDESTRUCTIBLE HEALTH

How I survived a car crash & healed myself so I could walk, climb, cycle and dance again

This guide will show you how and why to increase your usable oxygen. It follows my popular talk 'Exposing Oxygen: the power and extent of the role of oxygen in healing the body'.

My aim is to enable you to change your health experience, to bring you more into the present, to defuse old patterns, and enjoy your life right here, right now.

How to create indestructible health by opening yourself to absorb as much oxygen as possible and to make that oxygen available to all the cells inside your body.

By eating at least 50% raw food, breathing fully through every experience, drinking 6–8 glasses of water a day, focussing your thoughts by choice, learning to deal with old fears, choosing nurturing friends and environment, medicines that do no harm, exercise that you are happy with, fresh air and most of all loving yourself, you can grow into a new being – a person you love and respect as never before.

Credentials, influences, experiences

So let's get to the practical stuff. I am going to give a short explanation here. The full process of my discovery that a system was at work in my life, is in my title: 'Indestructible Soul: How I decided not to die', which is on Amazon and Kindle, in which I describe the accident where my leg was crushed, my near death experience, survival and recovery, leading to my exploration of why I survived against the odds. The material here is partly gleaned through that experience and also through treating many breathwork clients (in the 23 years since I qualified) and physically injured people (since the accident in 2000 and further training in 2002).

Many years ago I started a lifetime process, of making my health indestructible, through aiming to use my limited resources well, wishing the best health for my daughter, and self respect, that upon reflection had started after some physically challenging childhood experiences. I am forever grateful for my parents respectful way of treating me, that I believe led to my uncomplicated approach to caring for my wellbeing. So when I had a huge challenge as an adult, in the form of being crushed by a car, my physical body coped and my psyche was tough. I believe that what I was able to learn is beneficial to all those seeking to ease pain in their lives.

Building your Indestructible Health System

Here are some of the factors that I have become aware of. The physical result of them is the increase of available oxygen reaching each cell in the body.

1 Breathing fully
2 Drinking water
3 High raw food intake
4 Exercise
5 Supportive medicines
6 Careful choice of thoughts
7 Loving people
8 Sunshine and fresh air
9 Deep tissue injury treatment (to remove damaged cells, and renew blood vessels)

1 Breathing fully

Let's begin with the most fundamental and least understood method by which the body cleanses itself. Westerners breathe approximately 50% of the time. The rest of the time we hold our breath, out of habitual stress or fear.

In the breath we expel 70% of the toxins that the body must remove to maintain health, so by breathing more fully we can help ourselves a lot. Western birth practices lead us to be under abnormal stress just as we learn to breathe (by cutting the cord too soon, effectively asphyxiating the baby, as it has not learned to breathe yet). This causes holding of the breath as a stress response throughout life. This is why I learned to teach breathwork.

Take some time each day to focus on breathing fully, this may be during yoga, bathing, driving, meditation, eating or while going to sleep. Once you become aware of your breathing, you will notice when you are depressing it, and then you can remind yourself to breathe more fully again. I notice that many people hold their breath while thinking about a challenging problem, really just the time when we need all the oxygen we can get!

So number 1 is part of bringing more oxygen into the body.

2 Drinking water

On its own, unadulterated, unflavoured, perhaps dechlorinated by leaving it to stand, tap water is just fine: 6–8 glasses a day. You can drink other things, just don't think of them as water. If you drink coffee or alcohol be aware that they dehydrate you, so you will need more water.

Think of it as your body's cleaning system, much like washing clothes, would you expect them to get clean if you washed them in tea, or fruit juice?

Our bodies need water to balance the system, it is as basic as our need for oxygen, when no other gas will do. Water is used to balance the salt in the body, of which we also need enough, contrary to popular opinion. The blood will serve its function if the raw materials are available. For example, its viscosity must be correct for blood to reach the furthest cells from the heart, down the smallest capillaries ($0.05–0.08\mu$m). They are minute.

If you feel unwell or have a headache, the most supportive thing you can do for your body is to drink a glass of water.

Number 2 is about distributing the oxygen.

3 High raw food intake

Raw food is recognisable by the body, which was of course designed to consume produce uncooked. For about 25 years I ate 50% raw food. My health was extraordinarily good, and this helped me to survive and then recover well from my accident. It is relatively easy to eat this amount of food raw without a drastic change in lifestyle. In recent years, some people with serious illnesses are turning to raw food, to treat them and make them well again. It is interesting to see that once we stop poisoning ourselves our bodies will heal, from even quite severe problems. Logically it would seem that we are designed to eat a majority of fresh green shoots and leaves, and this is now what is recommended for an increase in vitality. Raw foods contain the enzymes necessary for digestion and absorption, enabling the body to use efficiently what has been eaten. It is estimated that between 15% and 80% of the nutrition is destroyed by cooking.

You may be relieved to know that raw means below about 45 degrees C, 117 degrees F, which means that you can warm soups, dry Kale to make crisps, dehydrate many familiar dishes rather than frazzling them. It's a new way of preparing food, and quite exciting. I am really enjoying it.

How raw food helps oxygen to reach all the cells, is specifically by enabling the body to maintain the correct alkalinity/acidity balance for health, cooked foods change this and create too much acidity in the body for adequate oxygen absorption. The only part of your body that functions in acidity is your stomach, to aid digestion. NB White processed flour and sugar create acidity in the whole body.

Number 3 is about enabling the body to use the oxygen.

4 Exercise

Part of the reason exercise is so good is that it helps with 1. Exercise speeds up the circulation, raises the breathing rate, raises the blood pressure, in doing so it can help the blood to reach places in damaged areas where the blood flow is usually restricted due to an old injury. This is one of the reasons that an aching part can sometimes feel better after exercise. Fast moving blood cleanses and clears the blood vessels.

Number 4 is about bringing more oxygen into the body.

5 Supportive medicines

Medicines that are designed to assist healing speed up the body's own healing mechanisms and place no additional strain on the body. These include certain foods (eg apples, garlic, onion, honey, almonds, pumpkin seeds), herbs and homeopathic remedies, also manual therapies that increase the blood and lymphatic flow. Taking a moment to breathe well, will often show that the problem is to do with being under too much stress, and letting ourselves wind down will give the body an opportunity to heal itself.

Vitamin C is the most powerful medicine we can use, it enables us to absorb maximum oxygen as it reaches the blood, and it removes toxins. As a preventative it is of course best taken by eating fresh, raw food. (It is destroyed by heating and we cannot store it in the body.)

Let me explain for a moment how the healing system works in the body.

There are two systems that operate in the body: the sympathetic and the parasympathetic. The sympathetic system comes into play when there is danger, and is operated by hormones such as adrenaline, which enables all systems to operate at maximum for the fight or flight response (opening large blood vessels and constricting smaller surface ones – hence going pale with fright). This system is supposed to be short term, only needed in emergencies, and self limiting. The parasympathetic system comes into play when the emergency has passed, the body goes into rest and repair mode, to restore tissues to normal loading and activity. It is supposed to work at night, enabling us to sleep and recover. The blood pressure naturally drops, the heartbeat and breathing rate slows down. For various reasons relating to our traditions of child rearing and lifestyle we spend far too much of our time under stress in sympathetic mode, thus stymying our body's attempts to repair and recuperate itself. This is partly what has lead us to believe that our bodies are not able to repair themselves. [Search on the internet for diagrams to show these 2 systems.]

Number 5 works by keeping dangerous substances out of the blood, thereby reducing the load on the system during illness.

6 Careful choice of thoughts

Our expectations govern our optimism, our hopes govern our heart rate, breathing rate, and as discussed in the previous section, our ability to repair our bodies. Being aware of how powerful these mechanisms are, can encourage us to become aware of when we are worrying about something that may never happen, which is causing our body to behave as though we are being stalked by a lion, when we are actually safe. These are habits that can be changed. (Using a breathwork or meditation technique will help you with this.)

Number 6 works by ensuring that our bodies are only under stress when there really is cause to raise our blood pressure.

7 Loving people

I chose these words deliberately, to suggest both being aware of the company we keep, and making sure that we are indeed, loving. Loving is a way to increase our health, by the joy we experience and the presence we feel, when we are surrounded by acceptance. This means that we spend more time in the parasympathetic state which enables our bodies to repair.

Number 7 works by allowing blood to reach the smaller blood vessels, and so the farthest outreaches of the body, enabling repair.

8 Sunshine and fresh air

The oxygen in a closed space gets gradually used up (there is about 12% in the air). Have you noticed how you start to yawn after being in a room with lots of people for a while? Yawning is your body's way of expelling stale air and refreshing itself, with a big breath of new air. Having a window ajar as you sleep fends off grogginess when you awaken in the morning. Sunshine is essential for health, physical and mental health. Apart from the obvious vitamin D that we gain by having some skin exposed to the sun, storing this vitamin up is what keeps us cheerful through the winter. Sadly peoples' natural inclination to enjoy the sun has been turned to fear and distrust, when in fact it is a major factor in wholesome health.

Number 8 works by providing more oxygen for use by the body.

9 Deep tissue injury treatment (to remove damaged cells, and renew blood vessels)

It is my understanding that pain is caused by areas of injury receiving insufficient oxygen to enable healing to take place.

This system: Deep Tissue Injury Treatment, that I designed after my accident and working on others with similar injuries, uses carefully directed force to break down scar tissue* and adhesions** that are blocking normal blood flow, thus clearing the way for oxygen to be supplied to damaged tissue for repair. The specific difference from other treatments is that both ends of each muscle concerned are worked on, as well as the centre, so that the whole length of the muscle gets cleared. If you think of the tension when you pull on a rope, or on knitting, the effect is not only on the part that you pull, each end of the fibre will be affected. Thus, when a muscle is injured each attachment is affected, and needs to be cleared of damaged cells to enable a new flow of blood.

Number 9 works by removing damaged cells that are blocking blood flow.

Use these techniques to increase the oxygen availability to every cell in your body, to grow and change into the person you feel you can become physically and emotionally. Increasing our available oxygen expands us in many ways.

Trust your body as an intelligent organism

Every single thing we put into our body (or onto our skin) either nourishes or challenges it in some way. If we consider this with everything we consume, we can live more healthily. For example, use whole foods rather than processed ones: that means any form of processing. We eat many products that have been developed and sold as 'better' for us e.g. bran flakes, gluten free foods, margarines; they aren't if they have been processed. Even the juices that are currently in vogue are processed. They can be very useful short term as medicine, and infinitely preferable to the chemical drugs that are freely consumed prescribed by our medical profession, sold to them by the drug manufacturers. However, they are not a complete foodstuff that your body can use as nature intended, as they do not have the whole food for the body to use. You get the idea? The closer the food is to the way it grew, the better your body is able to use it (if it is in fact, a suitable food, I mention the 'superfoods' currently recommended such as algae and wheat grass juice, which I do not consider natural foods for humans).

I wrote in a recent blog about realising that each ingredient in a recipe, should be something I would be prepared to eat on its own (obvious, I know)2. Mixing things together doesn't make them better for us, if they were unsuitable as foods on their own. I also realised that whatever I put on my skin I should be prepared to eat! If it gets absorbed into the skin it should be suitable as food. I'm not suggesting that we never do things that are unhealthy, what I am suggesting is that we are mindful on a daily basis of what we do to our bodies, for their long-term benefit. Our everyday habits are the ones that count in the long run. Just asking, 'How nourishing is this?' when we eat something, should start us thinking.

Health is a balance, the body has exquisitely sensitive facilities for monitoring and correcting all of its mechanisms (eg carbon dioxide, salt, calcium, enzymes, hormones) and if these are not working correctly, it is not because the body is faulty, it is because we are not giving it the raw materials it needs to correct itself.

Your body can clean itself, but only if it has the resources: specifically, enough water and Vitamin C. I once listened to an Analytical Chemist who spoke at a breastfeeding conference about heavy metals in the blood and breast milk. At the time chemicals in breast milk was a media issue. I was reassured by his matter-of-fact approach, trusting the body as an intelligent organism, to recognise what to expel. In his opinion the body could remove any toxin, given adequate intake of vitamin C.

How to begin

If you find you fall far short of how you know you should be living, your ideal scenario, try starting gently.

If you are drinking several cups of tea and coffee a day, and wine or beer, or fruit juice. Begin by drinking a glass of water in the morning and the evening.

If you eat very little raw food at all, begin with breakfast. Muesli with nuts, dried fruit and fresh fruit (The fresh fruit provides moisture or you can use fruit juice). Then try replacing biscuit snacks with fruit, the most luxurious ones you can think of. Have a look at some of the raw desserts you can make. These changed my life!

If you are feeling more daring, you could try 'Go Raw for a Day', Karen Knowler's free introductory PDF which gives you 2 day menus to try with all ingredients lists included. She has recently published 'Go Raw for a Week' which is a real paper book, if that's your preference. I suggest her, because although her recipes are slightly rustic, you don't need any special equipment to make them, and you will be familiar with all the suggested ingredients. There are many specialist raw food teachers for all types of specific ailments, my standpoint is for general health.

If you need to exercise, be creative, get a trampoline for your office! Something that is fun, join a group if running alone is not your thing. If running isn't for you at all, ride a bike to work or get off the bus a stop early and walk for 10 minutes. You really do not need to do a great mileage to stay healthy, if you combine it with eating well.

If you have frequent headaches, first of all try focussing on your breathing (especially out), drinking a glass of water, and eating some fruit. Then try a homeopathic remedy (perhaps Nux Vom if related to overdoing it, or Kali Bich if sinus-related), they are available in Holland & Barrett, Boots, Lloyds chemists and supermarkets. Regular exercise will help too. All of these things increase oxygen available to the brain.

There are videos on youtube and an explanation on my website of these:
*Scar tissue
**Adhesions

1 Full story available in my Interview on my youtube channel
2 I had a weird thought a while ago, on my blog.

Resources

If you would like to hear more about how my work changes lives, you can read their reports here. And if you'd like me to work individually with you to increase your strength and energy, please contact me and I will arrange to call you. I offer Rebirthing Breathwork sessions and a 3 month VIP programme to get your life on the path to Indestructible Health!

There is also an online programme that you can join to practice the tenets of Indestructible Health. See my website for details.

I had 13 years experience treating old injuries that resisted previous treatments at the Oxford Pain Clinic, developing my Deep Physical Injury Treatment system. I learned a great deal about what was possible from this time.

I teach the breathing technique, Rebirthing Breathwork, that makes you happy, helps you to change patterns that have been running since your creation. Ultimately you can use this every day, every hour, once learned it remains with you as your new way of breathing and experiencing life, enabling you to make choices about the company you keep and the way you earn your living, that are joyful and freeing. I believe that this practice saved my life when I lost half my blood in a few minutes when my leg was crushed by a drunk driver.

During my breath work training, I asked people if they'd like to live forever, and I couldn't find anyone that was enjoying their life enough to even consider it.

You can receive complete support in changing your life in these ways from me in a 3 month VIP programme on a one-to-one basis. This is a bespoke training, just for you, with all the tweaking you need to make it a perfect fit. Would you like to live forever?!

20 Breaths exercise

This is a useful pattern to use to breathe with more awareness:
The pattern is 4 short breaths and 1 long breath 4 times, until you have done 20 conscious breaths. Even doing

this once or twice a day will make a difference. You can find this on Youtube on video to be guided if you wish. You will also find a 40-minute guided breathing meditation on my Youtube channel.

Links to Further Reading:

Breathing Technique
Rebirthing Breathwork: Creating an Independent Adult, Catherine Holland Kindle PDF Paperback

Diet
Your Body's Many Cries for Water: You are not sick, you are thirsty. Don't treat thirst with medication! by Fereydoon Batamanghelidj
Karen Knowler, Go Raw for a Day, enables you to try eating solely raw for a day to see how it feels.
Easy Raw Main Meals, Kindle Catherine Holland
Russell James, The Raw Chef
The Reality of Breastfeeding, the perfect raw food for human infants. Kindle PDF

NB While Cow's milk is gradually being accepted as an unsuitable food for humans, do not just assume that the substitutes are better, e.g. Soya, which has many problems of its own and is not a healthy food unless it has been fermented.

Medicines
Pain & Trauma Recovery Catherine Holland, Old

Injury Expert
Confidently Refuse Vaccinations, on Kindle, Catherine Holland
abchomeopathy
British Homeopathic Association
Superjuice Me film Juicing for correcting disease, video introduced by Jason Vale. It is available free at the time of writing at www.superjuiceme.com

Contact Catherine Holland, please contact me for an exploratory call to work with me and see how to be the happiest person you can be.
catherine@catherineholland.co.uk

Twitter @joyousfreedom
Facebook Catherine Holland Indestructible Soul
Youtube Catherine Holland
Blog on my website www.catherineholland.co.uk

Thanks for reading, I hope you found this informative and inspiring. I wish you the very best of health!
Catherine Holland.

APPENDIX

How to write an affirmation and use the response column.

An affirmation is a phrase containing something we wish to affirm about ourselves, we won't see it as entirely true at the moment. It is something we wish to move towards, e.g. "I, Catherine, am now creating my ideal relationship", "I, Catherine, am now receiving in abundance; all my financial ventures are successes", "My confidence increases every day".
Be really bold, brave, poetic. Be specific. "My fame is spreading far and wide, for treating people and making them better". Something that feels outrageous!

It is said in the present as if it were already beginning, even if I have not met a suitable candidate yet; I am acknowledging that I am ready to begin a relationship and preparing myself. I write this out and my responses to it, as shown below, and then I continue to write it out in each of the 1st, 2nd and 3rd persons i.e.

I, Catherine am now creating my ideal relationship

You, Catherine, are now creating your ideal relationship

She, Catherine, is now creating her ideal relationship
Say them to yourself to see the effect you feel - a
reflection of others effectively condoning the change
you are making.

RESPONSE COLUMN

My affirmation here	**My response here**
I, Catherine, am now creating my ideal relationship	**I'm not ready**
I, Catherine, am now creating my ideal relationship	**I wish I could** etc.

Until I run out of different responses, perhaps 10 times.

Another example: The Universe has now prepared for me, Catherine, my perfect partner	**Oh, yes, where is he then?**
The Universe has now prepared for me, Catherine, my perfect partner	**Nobody would want me if they really knew**

me.

The Universe has now prepared for me, Catherine, my perfect partner

I don't believe it

The Universe has now prepared for me, Catherine, my perfect partner

I'd love that

The Universe has now prepared for me, Catherine, my perfect partner

Really?

It is useful to see the range of different responses I have to the same affirmation - there is a part of me that wants the change, and a part that resists it. I'm frightened that I might not be good enough, or I may make a mistake.

You may need to do this exercise several days running if you are making a major change. You can use your responses to create new affirmations if they indicate new material uncovered that you need to address, to proceed further with your intended change.

When working at personal growth, we often find that

processes to concentrate the mind are useful. Through the years we have developed some for areas covered in the book for use in small sharing groups, or with your rebirther. Here are a few examples:

Exercises

Communication
Think of 3 people in 3 different areas of your life eg work (a particular colleague), family (a parent perhaps or a sibling), relationship (your lover).
Write 3 words or short phrases for each to echo the type of communication that you have with each of these people in your life. Share these and see how they differ and if there are any repeated strands.

Think of 5 phrases you say frequently, to yourself to others or alone. What do they really mean? When you say them how do you feel, or what prompts you to say them?

Fear
Draw a mindmap. Take a sheet of paper and coloured pens. Write Fear in the middle with a ring around it. Around this put any situations in which you feel afraid, nervous or which you avoid, also in circles. Draw lines connecting them to the fear bubble, and to any of the other fears that they appear to be related to.

Phone up your Mum, ask her what you were afraid of

when you were little, really little. Do you remember any of these situations? Do they still make you afraid? What strategies did you develop for coping with these fears?

My story

I learned Conscious Connected Breathing as an adult. I used it initially to support me in living alone, having ended my marriage. It was an emotional healing journey. The most dramatic physical effect that I noticed at the time was the reduction in breathing problems. I was prone to asthma, in particular in reaction to the cold air. During one of my breathwork sessions I had a breath release, a dramatic relaxation of intercostal muscles; I felt as though my chest capacity had grown by a third. I could now ride my bicycle up a hill in the winter without becoming breathless. My children noticed that I had grown an inch taller.

However, another effect was only drawn to my attention recently, by working with a client who had been involved in a car crash. I, too, was hit by a car in the year 2000. I used the breath consciously for much of the time immediately following the accident and during my recovery period. I believe that it probably saved my life, as I was able to stay conscious at a time when I was severely injured, and to cope with challenging operations and painful healing processes. I have made an extraordinary recovery. Working with someone else who did not have this technique available at the time, has shown me how valuable it was to me.

BIBLIOGRAPHY/FURTHER READING

A GOOD ENOUGH PARENT Bruno Bettelheim

ASK AND IT IS GIVEN Esther and Jerry Hicks

CONVERSATIONS WITH GOD Neale Donald Walsch

CUTTING THE TIES THAT BIND Phyllis Crystal

I DESERVE LOVE Sondra Ray

LOVING RELATIONSHIPS Sondra Ray

MAGICAL CHILD Joseph Chiltern Pearce

PHYSICAL IMMORTALITY Leonard Orr

REBIRTHING IN THE NEW AGE Leonard Orr

REBIRTHING: THE SCIENCE OF ENJOYING ALL OF YOUR LIFE - now titled -

VIVATION: THE SCIENCE OF ENJOYING ALL OF YOUR LIFE Phil Laut and Jim Leonard

SPIRIT, MIND AND BODY - The Technique of Affirmation Mary and Ray Brooks
THE CONTINUUM CONCEPT Jean Liedloff

THE REALITY OF BREASTFEEDING Catherine Holland

THE WAY OF THE PEACEFUL WARRIOR Dan Millman

YOU CAN HEAL YOUR LIFE Louise Hay

ORGANISATIONS

British Rebirth Society
How to find a Rebirther in your area: many Rebirthers belong to the British Rebirth Society. You can find out if there is one in your area by visiting www.rebirthingbreathwork.co.uk or telephoning 0845 3308214
Do interview your Rebirther to find out whether you feel comfortable with them: Rebirthers vary in style a great deal.
It may be useful to find someone who has life experience that echoes your own in some way.

LLL La Leche League: Breastfeeding support from pregnancy through to weaning.
www.laleche.org.uk
General enquiries 0845 456 1855

NCT National Childbirth Trust: Childbirth and parenting charity offering antenatal classes, breastfeeding and postnatal support. Information on pregnancy, childbirth, breastfeeding and parenthood.
www.nct.org.uk
Breastfeeding helpline 0870 444 8708
Pregnancy and birth information line 0870 444 8709

Association of Breastfeeding Mothers: free telephone and internet support for breastfeeding mums.
www.abm.me.uk
0870 401 7711 9.30am - 10.30pm

Education Otherwise: a support group for families whose children are educated other than by attending school.
www.education-otherwise.org
eoemailhelpline@education-otherwise.org

Background:

A Rebirthing Breathworker for 26 years, Catherine has used the technique personally and to guide others in their personal and spiritual growth. Her experience has been useful during critical times in her life, ensuring safe passage through times of accident and stress, as well as in raising her three children. She has been honoured to work with an equal number of men as women, which is unusual in the personal growth industry. This gives her a unique perspective, an understanding that the emotional needs of men and women are the same, though their personality and circumstances will vary. Recovery from a road traffic accident has given her confidence for treating the physical as well as the psychological. She worked as a remedial injury specialist putting her experience of working with people to good use in all areas of her life. She has been a proofreader and editor and has written numerous articles for magazines and websites – including her own, and several books. "The Reality of Breastfeeding" was written from her experience of being a National Childbirth Trust Breastfeeding Counsellor for 19 years and a wish to continue to support mothers once she went to work full-time and was no longer available on the telephone during the day. She became interested in Rebirthing Breathwork when challenged in her relationship and seeking the courage to make necessary changes in her life. It had several extraordinary effects apart from the intended one including the disappearance of asthma. She is now in a relationship with spiritual growth at its centre, having found a man who wishes to journey with her. The story of this meeting is now published in a book: "That's Me! an email odyssey to find a soulmate", see website for details.

www.catherineholland.co.uk

Catherine Holland's published books:
Rebirthing Breathwork: Creating an independent adult

The Reality of Breastfeeding

That's Me! an email odyssey to find a soulmate

Indestructible Soul: How I decided not to die

eGuides
Stop Suffering Back Pain

Confidently Refuse Vaccinations

Easy Raw Main Meals

10 Keys to Unlocking Back Pain

10 Keys to Unlocking Neck Pain

10 Keys to Unlocking Hip Pain

10 Keys to Unlocking Ankle Pain

10 Keys to Unlocking Hand Pain

10 Keys to Unlocking Shoulder Pain

10 Keys to Unlocking Knee Pain

Catherine Holland is a Rebirther, trained with the Holistic Rebirthing Institute, and for many years a committee member of the British Rebirth Society. She has been teaching rebirthing breathwork for 26 years. She was a breastfeeding counsellor with the National Childbirth Trust for 19 years. She has three children. Following an accident where her leg was crushed by a car, she trained in Remedial Massage with the Northern Institute and founded a pain clinic in Oxford where she treated old injuries for 14 years. She is currently an inspiring author and Breath Coach. Information about her practice, articles and books can be found at www.catherineholland.co.uk

Printed in Great Britain
by Amazon

47486134R00088